ST. JAMES'S PALACE

My association with the Northwest Highlands has always been an extremely happy one and for many years I have visited the Loch Laxford area which is not far from Achfary. So it was a very pleasant occasion for me in 1979 to visit Highland Stoneware at Lochinver. I remember well the enthusiasm of the young staff, and I was fascinated by the way in which they had captured the spirit of the Scottish Highlands in the decoration of their pottery.

I am greatly impressed by the progress that has been made since then in the creative development of this product. The provision of much-needed employment has clearly been a great benefit to the area and has contributed much to the prosperity of the local community.

I would like to congratulate the pottery on its 25th Anniversary, and to wish all those who work there every success in the future.

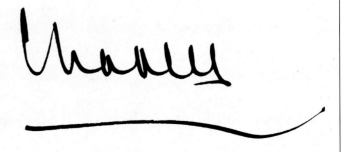

Sang de boeuf vase designed by Dorell Pirie, 14ins (35.5cms), 1998.

HIGHLAND STONEWARE

THE FIRST TWENTY FIVE YEARS OF A SCOTTISH POTTERY

Malcolm Haslam

The road to Lochinver.

Lochinver, the pottery in the near foreground.

RICHARD DENNIS
1999

ACKNOWLEDGEMENTS

The author and publisher would like to thank Grahame Clarke and David Queensberry for answering an endless stream of questions, and for sharing with us their memories of events, some of which took place over twenty-five years ago.

The staff of Highland Stoneware at Lochinver and Ullapool were always patient and helpful, ever ready to explain a technique or describe a process. Thankyou.

To Norah and David Grant we owe our special gratitude. They always ensured our comfort, both in the pottery and their home, and they gladly allowed us to disrupt their lives on many more occasions than we might reasonably have expected. We would like to congratulate David on maintaining such a comprehensive archive of documents and pots which offers so vivid a record of Highland Stoneware and the pottery it has produced.

We thank Mr M. Sales, Mrs Elizabeth Harris and her sons, Jonathan and Timothy, for allowing us to reproduce photographs of items in their collections.

We also thank Sue Evans, who has edited the book, for her expertise and patience.

Malcolm Haslam
Richard Dennis
1999

The Ullapool pottery and showroom.

Edited by Sue Evans

Photography by Magnus Dennis

Print, design and reproduction by Flaydemouse, Yeovil, Somerset

Published by Richard Dennis, The Old Chapel, Shepton Beauchamp, Somerset TA19 OLE, England

© 1999 Richard Dennis & Malcolm Haslam

ISBN 0 903685 73 6

British Library Cataloguing-in-Publication Data. A catalogue record for this book is available from the British Library

Cover: Pot and panel painted by David Grant, vase thrown by Paul Gow
End papers: tiles painted by Grahame Clarke

CONTENTS

FOREWORD

When I was in charge of the department of Ceramics and Glass at the Royal College of Art I felt that it was important, as far as possible, to equip students to continue with their work after graduation. The trouble was that many of the students were not clear what they wanted to do and of those who were clear, few had the talent and tenacity to be successful. This was not the case with David Grant who was not only clear about what he wanted to achieve but had the determination to make it happen.

David Grant's dream was simple, to set up a pottery in the north of Scotland making reduction stoneware using semi-industrial methods of production. The dream may have been simple but realising it was to prove extremely complicated. We agreed quite early on in the three-year course that David's work at the College would be dedicated to what became known as the Highland Stoneware project.

The idea of combining studio ceramic techniques, particularly reduction firing, with the industrial manufacture of pottery intrigued me and I became closely involved in the project. Grahame Clarke, David's tutor, and I both believed that Highland Stoneware was a viable proposition given David's drive and single-mindedness. Grahame was to be crucially important in helping David to design the range of products and develop the ceramic qualities that have given Highland Stoneware its distinctive character.

While David was a student at the Royal College the original range of products was designed and the manufacturing processes and ceramic qualities worked out. The business plan for the company was agreed and the necessary finance found. Grahame Clarke and I were so confident in the project that we became and still are investors and directors of the company.

Highland Stoneware is now a success story but the early days were difficult. It has survived and prospered in a period, particularly recently, which has been extremely difficult for the pottery industry.

When I first met David in 1971, I sensed a man of extraordinary determination who had a vision of what he wanted to achieve; this book is about that vision, how it was achieved and the people who made it possible.

The Marquess of Queensberry
1999

David Queensberry and David Grant
in the Highlands.

CHAPTER 1

GETTING STARTED

Highland Stoneware is now twenty-five years old. At 10 am on the 17th June 1974, the first meeting of the directors was held at 18 Fleet Street, London. The directors were David Grant, who had just gained his degree in ceramics at the Royal College of Art; Grahame Clarke, who had been his tutor; and Professor David Queensberry, head of the ceramics department at the College.

The idea of starting a factory in the Scottish Highlands for the manufacture of practical stoneware had taken root in the mind of David Grant some years earlier and was soon to become a reality. David was born on the 4th September 1948 in Achfary, a small village at the foot of Loch More, in the far north-west of Scotland. When the family moved thirty-five miles south to Lairg, he attended Golspie High School where he had his first experience of making pots, 'but I didn't go much for it', he was to confess some years later in an interview for a newspaper. Nevertheless, after completing a two-year general course at Duncan of Jordanstone College of Art in Dundee, he chose to study ceramics there.

At Duncan of Jordanstone, where he was a student from 1966 to 1971, David received a thorough grounding in the art and craft of pottery. Donald Logie, the head of department insisted that all his students acquired a sound practical knowledge of materials, equipment and processes. David has remained in touch with him and has often called on him for technical advice. Other people David met at the Dundee college were to play important roles in the history of Highland Stoneware. In 1967 he was first attracted to Norah Sullivan, a painting student,

and they would be married five years later. Paul and Rae Phipps were college friends who would later be the first to join David in Lochinver, and who would both be key figures in getting the pottery established. They are still with Highland Stoneware today. Another student, Linda MacLeod, would join the company as soon as she graduated from Duncan of Jordanstone, and she would quickly establish herself as a talented and influential decorator. Then there was Eric Marwick; they would meet again in London at the Royal College of Art, and Eric's later visits to Lochinver would usually prove both creative and festive! It was, too, at Dundee that David first met Peter Shipley, a kiln-builder from the Potteries who was visiting the College; his expert advice would prove invaluable on more than one occasion in the future.

While he was still a student at Duncan of Jordanstone, David wrote to Sutherland County Council and the Highlands and Islands Development Board to ascertain what financial assistance might be available to a young potter setting up in the Highlands. 'I agree with you,' replied the Sutherland County Council Planning and Development Officer on the 21st January 1970, 'that a working potter could be a considerable tourist attraction in addition to providing a reasonable living for the individual craftsman.' Towards the end of the year, an officer of the Highlands and Islands Development Board was writing to David about 'your plan to set up a commercial pottery in the Highlands'. Although the matter was deferred because David won a place at the

Slab-built stoneware dish made by David Grant at Duncan of Jordanstone College of Art, Dundee. With this piece, David won joint first prize in the Wenger Centenary Craft Pottery Competition, 1970.

David Grant with one of his stoneware sculptures installed at the Duncan of Jordanstone Diploma Show, 1970.

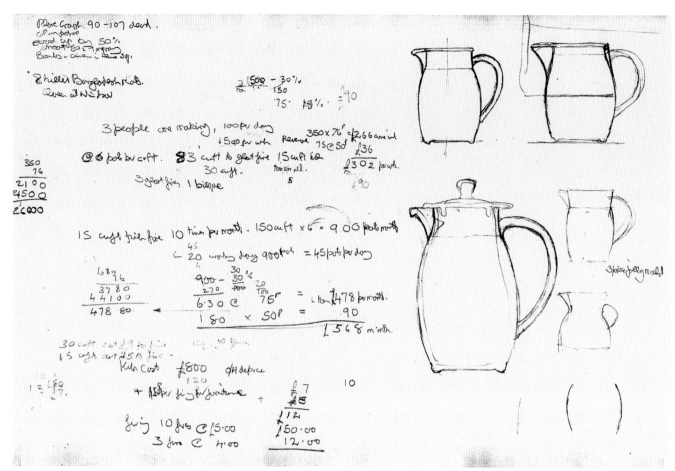

Page of drawings and calculations from a sketchbook used by David Grant during his second year at the RCA, 1972-73.

Royal College of Art, he would be in touch again with both institutions in the not too far distant future.

Within weeks of his arrival at the Royal College of Art in autumn 1971, David was working on the 'Stoneware Project'. When he had expressed his intention of making stoneware for table and kitchen, with the ceramic qualities of studio-pottery but using traditional industrial technology, there had instantly been a positive response from Professor Queensberry, the head of the department. It was his policy to combine the best practice of art and industry in his teaching. After a few years working in Stoke-on-Trent as a designer, Queensberry had been appointed to the post at the Royal College of Art in 1959, succeeding Professor Robert W. Baker who had always seen it as his job to provide the industrial manufacturers with the artistic talent which they thought that they required. Queensberry, on the other hand, considered that, rather than industry dictating to the College, the College should be offering inspiration and innovation to industry. He encouraged his students to follow their own inclinations, however radical, and at the same time to recognise the requirements of industry and experiment with industrial techniques and materials.

When Queensberry heard David's plans, he inaugurated the 'Stoneware Project'. A group of staff and students was to work on developing, manufacturing and marketing a stoneware range, and the members would meet from time to time to report progress and resolve problems. From the start, it was decided to adopt the jigger and jolley method of production, a traditional way of making pots in series which is, in effect, mechanical throwing, using plaster moulds. Knowledge of mould-making was provided by Grahame Clarke, one of the tutors in the department. As a student at the Royal College of Art between 1962 and 1965, Grahame had developed his mould-making skills while working with fellow student Martin Hunt (who in 1966 was to go into partnership with David Queensberry). Grahame had previously worked briefly for the studio-potter Harry Davis, who manufactured domestic stoneware, using some industrial techniques, at the Crowan Pottery in Cornwall until he emigrated to New Zealand in 1962. Before going to the Royal College of Art, Grahame had studied ceramics at Hornsey College of Art under Richard Parkinson, who was probably the first teacher in Britain to include industrial techniques in the curriculum.

David Grant spent his first year at the Royal College living in a Dormobile which he parked in Eric Marwick's garden at Clapham. In July 1972, David and Norah were married and when the new academic year started they moved into a flat in Holbein Place, near Sloane Square. Maybe as a result of a more settled existence or maybe because he now spent less time travelling each day, David was doing a lot of reading. A book which made a deep impression on him was *Design for the Real World* by the American designer Victor Papanek, published in London that year. Many of the ideas contained in Papanek's onslaught against designers, industrialists and advertisers were reflected in a paper entitled 'Criteria for Action' which David presented to a seminar in the Royal College of Art at the end of January 1973. David said that he had become disillusioned while making sculptures and murals during his last year at Dundee because he had been working for such a small elite. He wanted to concern himself with the practical needs of a wider public – a public who were being let down by a ceramics industry too obsessed with profit to provide a product with any real merit. Because the

materials used were over-refined in order to eliminate variation, and because production was over-mechanised in order to reduce costly and unreliable manpower, the public were forced to eat off bland and ugly crockery made by people whose work was humdrum and unsatisfying. To support his arguments, David quoted Siegfried Gideion and Mao Zedong, as students did in the seventies!

By 1973 the 'Stoneware Project' group had effectively shrunk to David Grant with Grahame Clarke providing technical assistance; Queensberry took a largely advisory role and could offer the benefit of his experience in the market-place. It was decided to use reduction firing and decorate the ware with celadon and tenmoku glazes originally developed by the Sung potters of ancient China. Trials were fired and moulds made. Gradually the range

Cup and saucer in the original shape designed by David Grant and made by him at the RCA, 1973.

Bowl in tenmoku glaze and jug in celadon glaze, made at the RCA, 1973.

Above: Promotion shot of some of the pieces in the original tableware range made at the RCA, 1973.
Above right: Group of pieces made at the RCA, including the first plate jolleyed by David Grant. The shape of the mug has been revived for one of the items used to commemorate Highland Stoneware's 25th anniversary.
Right: Production run of tableware pieces in celadon, supplied to Heal's store for market testing, 1973.

David Grant and his tableware at the RCA degree show, 1974.

began to appear and, in the summer, Professor Queensberry invited the buyers from the leading stores to come and see it. Most of them were enthusiastic, and Heal's agreed to market-test the range in the autumn. Before then, however, David Grant used a travelling scholarship to visit some of the leading stoneware manufacturers in Denmark. Partly as a result of this, it was decided to simplify some of the shapes.

Apart from his trip to Denmark, David took the opportunity while a student at the Royal College of Art to visit as many potteries as possible, to see what people were doing and how they did it. The College arranged visits to Stoke-on-Trent where David made several valuable contacts and renewed his acquaintance with Peter Shipley. On these visits, too, he started picking up second-hand tools and equipment which he stored either in a warehouse at Swadlincote, Derbyshire, or at Eric Marwick's place in Clapham. To find out about more rudimentary technology, David and Grahame went to see some traditional country potteries, including Thorburn's at Wetheriggs and Curtis the flower-pot maker of Ripon. David spent a day at Aldermaston with Alan Caiger-Smith who was helpful with good advice about how to operate effectively with a team of workers taking their turns at different jobs. Hans Coper, one of the tutors at the Royal College of Art, took him to meet Lucie Rie in

Albion Mews, where, no doubt, he was impressed by the orderliness of her workshop as well as the beauty of the pots she made.

David built a kick-wheel to a design by Hans Coper and always appreciated a talk with him over a drink and a game of bar-billiards. There were other people on the faculty at the College whom David found inspirational Eduardo Paolozzi sometimes collaborated with Grahame and David on experiments with different methods of decoration, and David admired his fellow Scot's energetic and practical approach to creativity. Another influence was one of the general studies tutors, Dominic de Grun, an ex-monk from Belgium, who had pieces of Oriental stoneware and loved good food. He was particularly interested in the relationship between pottery and food, how the preparing and eating of food often determined, and could also be enhanced by, the shapes, decoration and quality of ceramic utensils.

David Queensberry made a great impact on David's ideas and attitudes. The design consultancy which he operated in partnership with Martin Hunt at premises inside the Royal College of Art building, allowed David Grant to see for himself the professional way to deal with clients and make presentations. There he met Roy Midwinter of W.R. Midwinter Ltd., and Desmond Rawson

Group of bowls and dishes made by David Grant at the RCA, 1972-73, showing various decorative techniques; the pattern on the large dish was achieved by laying slip in the mould; the sgraffito decoration of the bowl on the left was admired by Hans Coper, then a tutor at the RCA.

of the Hornsea Pottery, two manufacturers who had both won international reputations for the design and quality of their tableware. On one occasion, when Peter Siemssen of Rosenthal was visiting, Queensberry suggested to Siemssen that after their meeting he might like to have a look at a stoneware range that one of his students had produced. Siemssen was impressed and cancelled his next engagement in order to inspect the ware more closely and discuss its commercial potential.

All the omens were good. The market-testing at Heal's had gone well, and David Grant spent much of his last year at the Royal College refining production techniques and preparing cost analyses and cash-flow projections; he was making an application to the Highlands and Islands Development Board for financial assistance. He gained his degree and in June 1974 Highland Stoneware (Scotland) Ltd. was incorporated. Capital was raised from a variety of sources including friends David scarcely realised he had! Then, on the 12th August, the Highlands and Islands Development Board wrote to David offering the new company a loan of £4,800 and a special grant of £3,000. Sutherland County Council found a site in Lochinver and agreed to build a factory. The dream had become a reality, and now the real difficulties would begin.

CHAPTER 2
EARLY YEARS

The situation in which David found himself towards the end of September 1974 was fraught with problems of time and place. The factory at Lochinver had to be built before production got under way, and until pottery was made and sold, money would be going out but none coming in. Originally, the Council scheduled erection of the prefabricated factory building on the Lochinver site for the autumn but, as we shall see, the timetable quickly started to slip. Delay was critical; the longer the delay the worse the crisis. There were orders to be met, and there was a plan to take space at the trade fair in Blackpool in February 1975. Meanwhile, there was an acute geographical problem. David was still living at the flat in Holbein Place, 700 miles from the factory site at

Lochinver, and equipment was dispersed between Stoke, Swadlincote and Clapham. Materials had to be ordered – and delivered where?

On the 26th September, David Grant, David Queensberry and Grahame Clarke met Peter Siemssen at the Royal College of Art and discussed an initial order from Rosenthal who were interested in selling the new tableware through their international chain of Studio Houses. Siemssen demanded some new items and several modifications to pieces in the basic range; samples were to be delivered to Germany by the end of December for consideration by the firm's international jury in January. The new shapes were designed by David and Grahame Clarke, working in collaboration; the additional items had

Grahame Clarke standing on the empty, windswept site at Lochinver, 1974. Perhaps he is looking for divine guidance, or he could be crying out: 'Why me, O Lord, why me?'

The factory at Lochinver was erected in February 1975, but it would be another four months before the electricity supply was connected.

to be modelled, and new handles and spouts had to be prepared for some pieces. It was another difficulty, on top of all the others. And Norah was seven months pregnant with their first baby!

For two years after leaving the Royal College of Art, David Grant kept a diary where he recorded the progress of Highland Stoneware and the setbacks which befell the new company. Some excerpts provide a vivid narrative:

'26.9 [same day as the meeting with Siemssen] Norah to station.' It had wisely been decided that Norah should stay with her family in Dunfermline while she had her child.

'28.9 To Gt. Missenden [Bucks]. M. Casson; collected clay, saw about kiln furniture.'

Mick Casson gave David his first bag of SMD clay – an important step towards developing the Highland Stoneware clay body. David then returned to London, packed and drove to Dunfermline where he arrived at 4 am. Travelling such distances, and keeping such hours, became the norm over the next few months.

'16.10 To Bradford, C&R Construction [the firm making the factory building] ...Sorted out a lot of building detail... Delivery in first week of November... Drove to Stoke.'

'17.10 ...Went walkabout to four Longton factories for an upright [jolley].'

'18.10 Kilns and Furnaces [kiln manufacturers]: Kilns ready to go... Payment: Half on delivery and rest when HIDB pay me... Drove to Swadlincote, left containers and machines, took Paul to Burton.'

Paul Phipps had decided to join Highland Stoneware, and now accompanied David on some of his trips. It had been something of an act of faith for Paul, who had a teaching job which, if it did not pay well, paid regularly. He was developing his own work and had recently sold a mural decoration, a composition of plates painted with geometrical designs, to the silversmith Gerald Benney. His technical ability, as well as his artistic talents, would be a great asset, and David was delighted when Paul agreed to join Highland Stoneware. The plan was that Paul and Rae, his wife, should move to Lochinver as soon as the promised living accommodation on the pottery site became available. Meanwhile, they stayed in their home at Errol, a village not far from Dundee where Donald Logie also lived.

'24.10 Heal's said they would launch Highland Stoneware when we were in production, press, poster etc. Very good idea. Bad news is Sir Paul Reilly's casserole split, so that is not so good.' (Sir Paul was President of the Design Council, which David hoped would give his tableware official approval. They did eventually, but not before Sir Paul had been presented with a new casserole!)

'4.11 Sales day... Harrods are taking it. Mrs Esamé [the buyer] said it was just what she was looking for; 48's of each order initially, so now issue is getting production rolling.'

'8.11... Still no action on site. House sites changed again, must go north. Collected upright jolley today, a good deal for Joe Hill at £60 and glad to have it... Drove north broke down, arrived Dunfermline 5am.'

Two days later, David met Gordon Kilgour in Edinburgh. Gordon had been living in Lochinver since 1972, and before that had worked for the earthenware manufacturers Buchan's at Portobello, just outside Edinburgh. He had served three-and-a-half years of a five-year apprenticeship and had learnt to mix clay and do jolleying as well as sometimes helping with firing the kiln. In Lochinver, he had worked with a local firm of builders and David had heard about him through the Sutherland County Council's planning department. At their meeting, David explained his plans and showed him the range.

'20.11 Rang C&R. They have stopped, started, stopped, and started and stopped again working on the factory.' (It is not hard to forgive the petulance that can be detected in this diary entry.) After a series of frustrating meetings with planners and builders in Inverness and Dornoch, factory and houses seemed no nearer completion.

'30.11 Baby daughter born today. Little attention paid to Highland Stoneware' is how the diary records the birth of Alexa.

Through most of December 1974 David and Grahame Clarke were busy at the Royal College of Art where they were making the samples for Rosenthal and Blackpool. On the 16th December, David despatched the first consignment and, the same day, heard that the green light had been given for work to start on the site at Lochinver. The factory should be erected in January.

Christmas and New Year saw but the briefest lull in activity, north and south of the border. On the 6th January David was disappointed to hear that work on the site had not yet started, but a week later he noted with satisfaction:

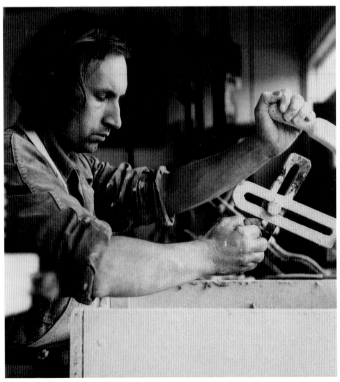

Gordon Kilgour started working at Highland Stoneware in March 1975; this photograph was taken not long afterwards.

'13th Jan... They're to start JCB work on site tomorrow. Hallelujah!'

There followed another visit to Stoke and a hectic round of factories and suppliers, trying to procure the tools and equipment that were still needed.

'16th Jan... Collected a lot of gear, motors, banding wheel etc. Took a whole morning but got all the tools I need, and these super huge glaze containers.'

'17th Jan ...drove miles for the second upright jolley. Got it, and a good enough buy, although a lot of setting up required. ...saw Peter Shipley, got pyrometer. Over to Swadlincote to unload.'

On the 25th January, David did not forget his literary heritage and organised a Burns supper after a hard day making pots at the Royal College of Art and packing up at Holbein Place. On the 29th January, his van loaded to bursting, he left London. After another busy day or two in Stoke, he arrived late in the evening at Blackpool where he 'ate a bad expensive meal and painted up the stand'.

The trade fair at Blackpool, the last to be held there, lasted from the 2nd to the 6th February and was an enlightening experience for David. He learnt quickly how to sell his wares and made many valuable contacts. Although the first day was 'basically much quieter than I thought or hoped', the last was a 'surprisingly busy day', and orders were taken from some important clients including Heal's, Harrod's and Keeg's of Seattle. Considering Highland Stoneware were not yet in production (and did not know for certain when they would be), there can be little doubt that the buyers were impressed with what they saw, and most of them were quite accommodating about delivery dates.

After visits to Dunfermline and Errol, David was in the Highlands again, staying with his mother at Lairg and spending his days on the site where at last things were happening. On the 18th February the 'building was unloaded by lunchtime and they were just starting to erect when I arrived... By evening a lot was up, with beams slung over.' A week later, 'I worked on fixing the roof, screwing down the roof plate, and finished in the darkening'.

On the 10th March, Gordon Kilgour started work. He had spent a week in Stoke-on-Trent during February, where David had arranged a crash course for him on plaster moulds and how to use them. At Lochinver, however, his work for the moment was finishing off the building and building shelves. At the end of the month, David drove south again to collect up more equipment from London and Stoke; then, with Grahame, he drove back to Scotland, picked up Paul at Errol, and eventually reached Lochinver:

'30th [March]... Arrived and made ourselves as at home as we could. GRC and Paul quite impressed.'

There remained, however, an enormous drawback to life and work. There was no electricity. David's calls to the Hydro Board whose job it was to bring power to the site, became ever more frequent and more urgent, but to no

The Pioneers. From left, Gordon Kilgour, David Grant, Paul Phipps, Rae Phipps, Grahame Clarke, with the factory behind. The photograph was taken in 1975.

David Grant at Lochinver, 1975, finishing a bowl on a kick-wheel that he made to a design by Hans Coper.

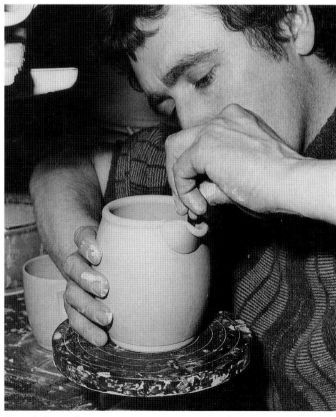

David Grant luting a spout onto a jug, Lochinver, 1975.

15

Paul Phipps glazing, Lochinver, 1975.

Linda MacLeod decorating, with a view of Loch Inver behind her, c1980.

Plates, 8ins (20.5cms), made at Lochinver in 1975 and decorated by Paul Phipps. Although the designs are essentially geometrical some leaf motifs make a stealthy appearance; sets of these plates were arranged on the wall in diamond shapes at the Eden Court Exhibition in Inverness.

avail. Without power, the machines would not function, and without machines no pottery could be made. The kilns used propane gas, but there was nothing to put in them. Grahame and Paul worked on the moulds; David arranged delivery of materials and tried to catch up on the paperwork; Gordon worked on the building. No-one was ever short of a job, but the lack of electricity was a serious problem. Another was the weather – bitterly cold and masses of snow. Roads were blocked and deliveries were delayed. On the 12th April, they had run out of plaster but the snow had cleared, so David and Grahame went to Stoer, a few miles up the coast, and took a long walk to the Old Man, a tower of rock standing a few yards out to sea from the cliffs. 'Really impressive,' David noted in his diary, 'blew away the cobwebs.'

The next day came welcome news: 'Rosenthal order uplifted all,' David wrote, 'orders boosted considerably –

about £3,000 to £3,500 worth.' Renewed confidence can be detected in a diary entry two days later: 'Place already coming round and looking like a pottery more and more.' But there was still no electricity.

On the 11th May, David wrote to Queensberry:

'We still lack electricity and the board are not due to begin work until 20th May. This is despite the M.P. [Robert McLennan] contacting the head of the Hydro Board, which brought us forward to a three week wait rather than ten to twelve weeks after paperwork had been completed. It is a severe handicap, but we are still busy multiplying moulds. With the damp atmosphere we have had quite a lot of plaster being winded, causing master moulds to stick and break, but we are getting through it with paraffin heaters on constantly.

The building looks really fine now. We have the showroom ³/₄ completed, and the machines painted. There are very few visitors around at present, but undoubtedly we have lost out, as it will take us so long to build up stocks... Slowly the place is taking shape. I am remaining optimistic, sober, and quite enjoying solving the problems.'

The Hydro Board duly started work on the 20th May but there were further bureaucratic obstacles and technical hazards to be overcome and it was not until the 30th May that David was able to write in his diary: 'Magic old day that the power came on.' On the 2nd June he recorded: 'Actually made some soup bowls today.' There were still problems; some of the machines broke down almost as soon as they were switched on. But at last everybody was doing what they had come to Lochinver to do – make pottery. Grahame came up again when the Royal College of Art term ended and on the 16th June David wrote in the diary: 'Nice to have Grahame walking around making things work.' The kilns were fired, and although the first results were not brilliant, some fine tuning solved the problem. Finally, the important day arrived:

'14th [July] Opening day. Took a few quid and very nice to see some pieces of pottery being sold at last.' He noted a demand for cream jugs, and the entry ends: 'Also evident that we need decorated pieces.'

Common Milkwort
Fort George 1840

Above: In search of inspiration, David Grant bought this postcard of a watercolour painted in 1840 at Fort George, showing the Common Milkwort. It was the source of much early Highland Stoneware decoration including the *Celadon Floral* pattern.
Right: Tableware decorated in the *Celadon Floral* pattern is here combined with pieces of the plain *Celadon*.

Early floral decoration painted on plates, 10ins (25.5cms), 1979-80. The plate on the left is one of the earliest in the HS40TT glaze; the others are Lochinver glaze.

From left: Plate, 10ins (25.5cms), decorated with a floral design by Linda MacLeod, and an experimental design by Grahame Clarke, both c1977.

David Grant decorating at Lochinver, 1977.

It had always been the intention that Highland Stoneware should manufacture a range of utilitarian pottery covered with subtle, but plain, glazes. The principal reason for this was that costs would be kept to a minimum and therefore a wider public would have the opportunity to enjoy a quality product. But the best intentions are so often the least appreciated. Demand for the tenmoku glazed tableware was never strong, and, partly due to technical problems with the glaze, production was phased out within a year or two. The

Table-setting of pieces decorated in *Lochinver*. The pattern was introduced in 1979, at the same time as the pale blue glaze on which it was painted.

Rae Phipps working in the factory showroom, Lochinver, 1975; *Celadon*, *Tenmoku* and *Culag* are on display.

Group of early Highland Stoneware workers, 1977. From left, Robin Noble, Katie Graham, Grahame Clarke, Bella Langlands, Diarmid MacAulay, Linda MacLeod, Ian Friar, Ishbell McLennan, Paul Phipps, Gordon Kilgour, David Grant.

Early staff at Lochinver, 1975. From left, Paul Phipps, Norah Grant, Rae Phipps, Gordon Kilgour, David Grant, Barbara Mattner.

From left, Barbara Mattner and Rae Phipps in the factory, 1975.

19

The Highland Stoneware workforce, 1979. From left, Elizabeth Templeton (office), Bush Campbell (behind), Linda MacLeod, Katie Graham (behind), Paul Phipps, David Grant, Gwen Richards, Sheila Matheson, Ian Friar (behind), Gordon Kilgour, Christopher MacLeod (behind), Duncan Campbell.

celadon glazed tableware always sold much better, and it continues to sell well today, but demand has always been steady rather than overwhelming.

The people that visited the showroom on the 14th July 1975 were readier to buy the decorated ware than the plain. There were only a few decorated pieces on sale, and they were only displayed because the quantities of celadon and tenmoku that there had been time to make before opening day had not been sufficient to fill the shelves. Paul Phipps had brought some decorated pieces with him from Errol, and they were pressed into service. When they had been sold, people were asking for more. Everyone quickly realised that a rich source of income, while so much production capacity was taken up on the big orders for celadon and tenmoku tableware, would be decorated pieces sold from the shop. And David was quick to develop this unexpected side of the business. Entries in the diary soon start to record decorating in progress, usually for shop stock, and on the 18th September, David complained: 'Not really getting down to decorating for the Aviemore show.' The trade show at Aviemore, held every October, is an opportunity for the retailers, mainly from Scotland, to see what merchandise is available for sale to the millions of tourists who visit the Highlands each summer. It had been decided to show decorated as well as plain ware on the Highland Stoneware stand.

Everybody contributed to the new development. Paul was an accomplished decorator in what was irreverently referred to as the 'Hara-ho!' style of Oriental brushwork – lines, flicks and blobs which translate into stems, leaves and petals. Grahame had his own version of the 'Immortelle' pattern made famous by Royal Copenhagen, and this was rendered more suitable for Highland Stoneware by substituting the thistle for the immortelle and calling the design *Culag* after a locality just south of Lochinver village. Another early decorative motif that Grahame introduced was the fishing fly which represented one of his own passions and had a clear local relevance. David rang Donald Logie at Duncan of Jordanstone and asked about the possibility of Linda MacLeod visiting Lochinver and trying her hand at some decoration. She stayed a couple of days, did 'some nice painting', as David commented in his diary, and the next year came to work permanently for Highland Stoneware, as soon as she had graduated from art college.

David reported on the Aviemore show in a letter to Grahame in London, written on the 27th October 1975: he wrote that there had been 'a lot of admiration for the Culag pattern.' It was a very successful fair for Highland Stoneware. Over thirty new accounts were picked up, mainly craft-shops in Scotland. Decoration was now firmly established, and in December the Eden Court Conference

Alexa makes her move! The Prince of Wales, having just had his kilt tugged by the MD's daughter, warns the young lady of the risks she is taking.

The Prince of Wales signing the Highland Stoneware visitors' book, 1979. David, Paul and Katie Graham hover.

The Prince of Wales tries his hand at decorating while Linda admires his skills.

Highland Stoneware jug, decorated by the Prince of Wales, with his own design, 1979.

Centre in Inverness organised an exhibition there of dishes painted by David, Paul and Grahame. In 1976, David worked on floral motifs, keeping an eye open for any sources of inspiration. In February, he visited London to give a talk to students at the Royal College of Art, and he took the opportunity to browse in Harrod's where he was delighted by the display of Highland Stoneware; he was also impressed by 'some beautiful prints in the Natural History Museum.' Calling one day on his old friend Patience Macgregor at her craft-shop in Bonar Bridge, he bought some postcards she had had printed of drawings, done by one of her forebears, of local wild flowers. He wanted to make Highland Stoneware decoration relevant to the area, both through the choice of motifs, and by using local minerals in the pigments.

In 1976 the *Celadon Floral* pattern was developed and used on tableware as well as purely decorative pieces. *Celadon* and *Celadon Floral* were marketed in combination – plain tableware sets with the larger pieces such as coffee pots and casseroles painted with the pattern. The strong tone of the celadon glaze effectively restricted the range of colours which could be used for the patterns, so in 1978 Grahame started working on a paler, bluer glaze on which the pigments showed up in soft pastel tones. The glaze was called 'Lochinver', and Linda devised a floral pattern (also named *Lochinver*) exploiting the new possibilities.

David Grant with Charles Rennie, a marketing officer of the Highlands and Islands Development Board, on the company's stand at a trade fair in Atlantic City, USA, 1977.

Stuart Grant, aged four, offers a helping hand to Linda as she decorates a cheese dish with the *Lochinver* pattern, 1980.

Aerial view of the pottery, 1977. In the foreground are the wooden cabins where the Grants and the Phipp's lived for four years. Left of the factory is the caravan which Linda occupied, and to the right is Alexa's playpen. Oliver Ross's bus is backed up to the factory door, loading tableware to carry to the railway at Lairg on the first leg of its journey to Hamburg, London or New York.

Linda proved herself a talented decorator and designer of patterns. Soon after joining Highland Stoneware, she started painting special pieces, including a view of the Free Church at Lochinver which in December 1976 was offered as a Christmas gift in *The Scotsman*. Her imagination was rich in slightly offbeat themes, and when the opportunity was provided by a second Christmas show at the Eden Court Centre, she presented a series of dishes painted with delicately drawn fantasies.

Meanwhile, production at the factory was becoming more and more efficiently organised. Gordon Kilgour grew steadily more skillful and was soon an accomplished maker. In 1978, a local lad, Christopher Campbell, was taken on to assist him and Bush, as he is known, has remained with the company ever since. At the same time Sheila Matheson, from Lairg, was taken on and trained as a decorator; she would stay for fifteen years with Highland Stoneware. Other employees, many from the surrounding area, came and went, some more permanent than others. There was Barbara Mattner, a German girl who appeared at the factory not long after it had been built; she was hard-working and efficient and could turn her hand to anything, from dusting and scrubbing to helping Paul with the kilns. Another was Katie Graham, a strong-charactered lady who had worked as a nanny; she dusted the biscuit wares after they came out of the oven and fixed handles and spouts on jugs and bowls.

Orders continued to flow in, big and little, from the U.K. and abroad. Macey's of New York placed an order in the first few months; Harrod's made a repeat order within days of taking delivery of their first. David was gratified to learn that Philip and Lavinia Rosenthal used Highland Stoneware in their own dining room at their home in Bavaria. Another, even more prestigious seal of approval was set on the enterprise when H.R.H. the Prince of Wales visited the factory in July 1979.

Highland Stoneware was one of the places Prince Charles was taken by the Highlands and Islands Development Board chairman, Sir Kenneth Alexander, on an official tour. He had a long chat with Gordon, Linda helped him paint a jug with the Prince of Wales's feathers, David explained how everything worked, and Katie presented him with a commemorative dish designed by Grahame (feathers again). He bought some pieces for himself and some presents for Princess Anne and the Queen Mother. But the incident which delighted the press was when little Alexa gave an inquisitive tug at the royal kilt. *The Scotsman* reported: "'I wouldn't do that,' [the Prince] told her with a chuckle. 'It might be dangerous.'" He stayed longer than scheduled, and followed by his ADC and a bevy of Highlands and Islands Development Board officials, he was away.

CHAPTER 3

EXPANSION

Towards the end of 1979, a new glaze was developed by Grahame Clarke. Known as HS4OTT, it has been used as the ground for most of the decoration on Highland Stoneware since it was introduced. It is a soft grey, and it has the quality of a blank canvas; any colour looks well against it. The first designs to be painted on it were the *Blue and White Specials*, a group of pieces executed about 1980 by Linda MacLeod, Grahame Clarke and others. Blue and white decoration required the neutral grey ground, and could never have been used successfully on the blue-green celadon glaze or the pale blue Lochinver. A blue and white pattern called *Culkein* (the name of a bay not far from Lochinver) was developed by Grahame for tableware. Its classic simplicity reflects the work he had lately been doing for the Danish firm of Bing and Grondahl. Another tableware pattern introduced in 1980 was *Elphin*, named after a small hamlet on the road between Lochinver and Ullapool. Developed by Linda and David it featured the dog-rose, a wild flower growing in abundance locally, on the serving pieces (teapots, casseroles and cheese dishes etc.), while other pieces in the range were painted with a minimal leaf motif.

In 1979, Highland Stoneware were in a position to have decent living accommodation built for the Grants and the Phipps's. The wooden cabins which had been their homes since 1975 had not been altogether satisfactory. There were now five Grants, Stuart (b.1976) and Jennifer (b.1978) having joined David, Norah and Alexa, and three Phipps's, Paul's and Rae's son Graham having been born in 1976, and the cabins were hardly appropriate and certainly not spacious enough dwellings in which to bring up young children. Atlantic gales are not a rare feature of the weather in those parts, and in the high winds the cabins threatened to take off. As David noted in his diary on the 5th September 1975: 'They really wobble in the increasing winds.' But moving into larger, more solid housing was not just a matter of physical comfort; it gave a feeling of permanence and helped to turn the pottery into a community. David Queensberry visited Lochinver the following summer, and on his return to London he wrote to David Grant:

> 'I thought the houses were fantastic and it is really good to see that Highland Stoneware is now a little community that is making sense not only from the point of view of a production unit but also in social terms. It was, after all, very much that side of the business that attracted you to it in the beginning.'

Meanwhile, the pottery had been more or less accepted by the larger community, the villagers of Lochinver. At first, relations had been strained. The factory had been built on land which had been supposed to have been earmarked for a children's playground. But, with a conscious effort, the potters found their place in a society which came to accept them with generous friendliness. David's father, Johnnie Grant, had been known to some of the villagers, and that helped. So too, of course, did the jobs which Highland Stoneware offered and the tourists whom the pottery showroom attracted. For many years David and Paul would take a wheel to the Assynt Games, held in the village every summer, and the local children were given the opportunity of throwing a

Lack of space at the Lochinver factory is evident in this view of the glazing area, 1980 – it also shows the decorating area and the plaster workshop.

Gordon Kilgour amid the congestion of the assembly area, which appears almost to overwhelm him. By 1980, a larger factory at Lochinver was becoming imperative.

The unit at Ullapool was built in 1981. Its location, on the edge of the town, is much less isolated today than it appears here.

The 90 cubic feet kiln was kept well wrapped up while the new Lochinver factory was erected around it. The Grant's house, built in 1979, can be seen in the background.

Building works at Lochinver became totally disruptive during the winter 1982-83. Partly laid floors, rubble and dust made production impossible.

pot. In 1977, David first organised another activity for the Lochinver young; on one day each year, schoolchildren are invited to the pottery to paint a plate for the Save the Children Fund. As well as helping a good cause, the event has promoted the integration of the pottery into the community.

Although living conditions at the pottery had improved, and the pottery itself was now more readily accepted by the people of Lochinver, lack of space in the factory building was becoming a serious problem. At first this had been particularly aggravating while a large order was being packed up for despatch. When the first big Rosenthal order was despatched, it took an entire pantechnicon to take it away, and there just was not room for that much bulk in the factory – itself not much larger than a pantechnicon! But with ever-increasing production, lack of space became a day-to-day difficulty. In a letter Grahame Clarke wrote to David on the 26th June 1980, he focused on a particularly worrying aspect of the problem:

'One of our basic techniques is the making of pottery from plaster moulds... Mould making... is probably the most neglected area, plaster behind the kilns, mixing amongst glazing and Linda's back, treading on Paul's toes, showering bits over the decorating pigments, plus turning and making moulds within an area 8 foot by 4 foot, two thirds of which is taken up with bench, storage and whirler. Absolutely ridiculous.'

In these circumstances, expansion was imperative. There had for long been the possibility of a second factory at Ullapool, thirty-seven miles to the south. The Highlands and Islands Development Board had acquired a site there for light industrial use, and in March 1976 they had urged David to expand there, and they had offered him their full support. There had been the customary delays, but now David chivvied and, on the 18th November 1980, the Board approved the plans of the new unit, and early the following year building was under way. David contacted Peter Shipley about a new kiln.

At the Lochinver factory, despite the cramped conditions, this was a period of new developments in decoration. Grahame had devised some new pigments which fired satisfactorily with the body and glazes. Among them were a bright turquoise and an intense matt white, and one clear frosty day in January 1981, when David was enjoying a brisk walk at nearby Achmelvich Bay, the waves rolling in were exactly the same turquoise, and the foam on their crests was matt white. The *Seascape* pattern was born. At about the same time, David, Grahame and Linda were all contributing to the evolution of *Landscape*, which developed from the tableware pattern *Assynt* and featured Suilven, the sugar-loaf mountain which dominates the scenery around Lochinver.

On the 28th June 1981, the Ullapool unit opened, although the kiln would not be installed until October. The road between Lochinver and Ullapool has, since then, been considerably improved, but in those days many more tourists visited the latter than the former. Moreover, Ullapool is a busy ferry terminal. So, the plan was that the Ullapool pottery should be a tourist attraction as much as a production unit. Here was enough space to have a large showroom, and visitors were encouraged to wander round and watch a thrower and decorators at work. Liz Hoey, who had been running her own pottery at Dornoch, was recruited to run the unit. She threw pieces specifically aimed at the giftware market for which the showroom at Ullapool was intended to cater. Another activity at Ullapool soon after it opened was the hand-pressing and painting of *The Highland Village*, models of crofts, houses, cottages and other buildings in Lochinver and elsewhere.

The Lochinver factory was by this time leaking like a sieve, and cracks had appeared in most of the walls. In October 1981, a site meeting was held and soon

Linda MacLeod painted this tile c1982, with the view from one of the factory windows. It shows a road being built to some council houses nearby.

construction was under way. Before the builders started erecting the new factory, however, the big new kiln was put in place. It would not have gone through the doors of the finished building, so the new factory was built round it. The new kiln had been acquired five years earlier. In October 1976, Peter Shipley informed David that a 90 cubic feet kiln he had recently built for a projected tile factory in High Wycombe was available because the venture had been aborted. He told David to offer a fraction of what it had cost its owners who were nevertheless quite happy to accept the offer. Its purchase was a good piece of forward-planning by David. The new kiln would more than double the pottery's capacity, and the two smaller kilns which had previously been used for both bisque and glost firing would now be used for bisque only. It had been stored at Stoke-on-Trent until it could be used.

The building work went on at Lochinver and by the end of the year production was seriously hampered. It was an opportunity to arrange a visit to Stoke-on-Trent for Gordon Kilgour and Bush Campbell. They had a new oval-headed jigger which they were having difficulties operating. David recognised, too, that first-hand experience of other people's methods and procedures could well be enlightening. The three of them arrived in Stoke on Monday the 28th February 1983 and were joined by Grahame. The next day they visited four suppliers, two museums and English Ironstone China, where they were given a complete tour of the factory and Gordon had a go on an oval jigger. At E.W. Goods, David bought some new decorating brushes, including some made exclusively for painting the gold line down the sides of Rolls Royces. On Wednesday, they toured more suppliers and another two factories and in the evening watched Stoke City draw 1-1

The new factory at Lochinver was erected round the old one. The Phipp's home, far left, had been built in 1979.

View of the pottery at Lochinver after completion of the new factory. The access road running behind the Grants' and Phipps's homes had to be built out into the loch, thus altering the coastline of Britain.

The winter of 1983-84 was severe in northwest Scotland. The new factory at Lochinver stands amid the frozen wastes.

Above: *Jig* decoration was introduced in 1983. A red-glazed bowl picks up one of the colours in the pattern.
Right: Linda MacLeod works on, impervious to the builder putting some finishing touches to the Lochinver factory.

Above: When David Grant gave a demonstration of decorating at Hall's department store in Kansas City, 1983, he found two fluffy-toy sheep made perfect models.
Right: A Scotsman abroad. On his way to Honolulu, David poses on a quay at San Francisco. Behind, Alcatraz floats in the bay.

Above: David Grant with the American potter Bob Flint, Honolulu, 1983.
Right: Home away from home! David Grant finds Suilven on the coast of Honolulu, 1993.

with Manchester United. Thursday was spent at T.G. Green's where they were allowed to roam around the factory and talk to anyone. Green's had supplied blanks to Highland Stoneware when it had been impossible to expand production capacity at Lochinver. 'Gordon and Bush,' wrote David in his report of the trip, 'were working on the semi-automatic and roller-head machines and really got in the swing – making hundreds of good pots for Green's!' David himself spent most of the afternoon with the head mould-maker, finding out about oval moulds. 'This was invaluable,' he wrote in the report. The next day they went home.

On their return, the new factory at Lochinver was nearing completion. At least, there were fewer trenches to

cross and drain-holes to negotiate, and most of the rubble was now outside rather than inside. It would still be some time before production was back to normal, but new glazes, pigments and patterns kept emerging. Grahame had produced a red glaze, and it was tried on some pieces of tableware as a contrast to others in the celadon glaze. Then David developed a new pattern called *Jig*, which was used on tableware sets with bowls in the red glaze; giftware in this pattern was named *Wallpaper* (an ironic allusion to a scathing remark from Grahame about some Highland Stoneware patterns). In homage to his revered Robbie Burns, David Grant designed the *Tam o' Shanter* range, with silhouette illustrations accompanied by a few lines from the ballad. Meanwhile, Linda started drawing hens,

Linda MacLeod shows off examples of *Hens*, c1984.

and no-one could stop her. Quite remarkable were the antics performed by Linda's hens – carrying umbrellas, walking on tightropes – even one impersonating the Reverend Robert Walker skating on Duddingston Loch in Raeburn's famous portrait.

The next pattern to be developed was *Sheep*. David had been asked to demonstrate decorating at Hall's, a store in Kansas City, U.S.A., which had bought large quantities of Highland Stoneware. To give his booth a Scottish flavour, two fluffy-toy sheep had been corralled, and David had found himself drawing them on the pottery. From there, the pattern slowly evolved, via Henry Moore's 'Sheep' sketchbook and the graphics on a jelly-baby packet. Demonstrations in stores had become a regular means of promoting sales. In the early 1980s, Linda had visited shops in Newcastle-upon-Tyne, Bristol, Buxton and London, and, in 1983, David went to Hawaii, where he demonstrated at Liberty House in Ala Moana as part of their two-week gala 'The Pageantry of Great Britain'. David always wore his kilt on these occasions.

If Highland Stoneware staff were out and about in Stoke-on-Trent and Ala Moana, the world was coming to Lochinver as well. Visits by performing artists in the village were always a great boost to morale, specially during the long winters when it sometimes became quite hard to believe that there was anything much beyond Suilven. In 1983, Leonard Friedman brought the Scottish Baroque Ensemble to Lochinver village hall at the end of a long, hard tour. A gale was blowing. But, as a reporter wrote in *ArtWork*, 'it was a triumph. Perhaps for all the incongruity of it, the best concert of all. They played with such startling perfection, there was nothing but the music.' Other visitors included the Medieval Players and the Scottish Opera-Go-Round.

After the *Landscape* pattern had been developed in 1981, and *Sheep* in 1984, there was some embarrassment when it was discovered that Grahame Clarke had apparently invented both on a plate that he had painted as early as 1975.

CHAPTER 4
CREATIVE ENERGY

The showroom at Lochinver, c1984. Linda MacLeod is on the right; most of the staff work in the shop from time to time. The decorators often gain useful tips from the comments that shoppers make about the designs.

By 1985, Highland Stoneware had established itself as a manufacturer of high-quality tableware and decorative ceramics, and the company's name was known and respected in the market-place. The labour-force had risen to twenty, divided between the two factories, and David Grant could easily have become engulfed in administrative and commercial affairs. But there were two other aspects of the business which had always seemed particularly important to him, technology and education. While still a student at the Royal College of Art in 1973, he had sketched a blueprint for 'the company as an educational structure, a constant investigation into the problems of manufacturing technology and industry, on all levels, with all who wish participating'. He had suggested that it was 'very important to make provision for research and development', and 'to have a fund set aside for educational travel for workers in the pottery'.

The Highlands and Islands Development Board had helped the company with loans and grants to start the pottery, and it had helped again when the Ullapool unit had been set up and the Lochinver factory rebuilt. The Board had assisted in promoting the product and training the staff. In 1979, the vice chairman, Rear Admiral D.A. Dunbar-Nasmith, had been largely instrumental in making it possible for Highland Stoneware to build houses on the factory site. The same year, it had been his imagination and energy which launched the Highland Craftpoint. Under the auspices of the Highlands and Islands Development Board and the Scottish Development Agency, Craftpoint provided marketing, development and training services to the craft industry in Scotland. David Grant had been on its Council from the outset, and Dunbar-Nasmith was chairman.

Sheila Matheson worked as a decorator from 1978 to 1992. She is seen here unpacking the 90 cubic feet kiln.

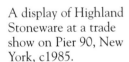

A display of Highland Stoneware at a trade show on Pier 90, New York, c1985.

The introduction of throwing at Ullapool had caused a problem. The SMD which Highland Stoneware had always used as a base clay had a springiness which made it less liable to stick to the moulds, but more difficult to throw on the wheel. Something had to be done about this clay anyway, because the seam from which SMD was dug had nearly been exhausted. Grahame Clarke did some research and developed a clay body which was suitable for both throwing and moulding. It had also emerged that some throwing skills needed developing, and Craftpoint provided some help in the form of George Dear, their ceramics officer. George is a potter of great experience and wide technical knowledge, and he not only helped with the throwing, but played a part in making improvements to the 90 cubic feet kiln at Lochinver. Craftpoint's policy of integrating industry and education was well implemented when, in October 1985, George Dear brought along Ian Pirie, head of the ceramics

department at Gray's School of Art, Aberdeen, with his oxygen probe analyser. Using this instrument, it was possible to control precisely the atmosphere in the kiln, and, in consequence the results of each firing were now more consistently of high quality. Another improvement in firing was effected by Tom Malcolm, a Highlands and Islands Development Board officer, who lined the kiln with fibre modules; this reduced firing times to about three hours, remarkably fast for firing reduction up to 1300°C. Such breakthroughs are not made without casualties; during one firing, David expressed an anxiety about fumes from the kiln. 'No problem!' said Tom, in a macho kind of way, and promptly passed out.

Highland Craftpoint fulfilled the educational aspect of its remit by running courses at its headquarters in Beauly, a village not far from Inverness. Instruction was given in skills such as mould-making, and Highland Stoneware

Three sizes of extruded fish dishes. From the top, special extra-large salmon dish 33$^{1}/_{2}$ins (85cms), standard salmon dish 25ins (64cms), and fish server 16 ins (40.5cms), c1993.

personnel often benefited. Technicians from Stoke came to Beauly to give demonstrations, and a stream of top studio-potters visited and gave talks about their work. In 1985, George Dear invited the American potter John Glick to come, and David Grant took along five of the Highland Stoneware staff. 'Glick,' Margie Hughto and Garth Clark have written,

'is one of the select cadre of functional potters whose example and free sharing of information have contributed to the rising standard of production pottery in the United States.' (*A Century of Ceramics in the United States 1878-1978* by G. Clark and M. Hughto, New York: E.P. Dutton, 1979)

David found the workshop inspirational. Glick's whole attitude to his work, and the dedication that he showed his craft, reminded David of his own aims and ideals. Moreover, Glick demonstrated a technique which was to become important to Highland Stoneware – the method of making pots by extrusion. David had been aware of the process, and it had been used in a handful of potteries in Britain, but now David realised that it was particularly applicable to the manufacture of serving-dishes for salmon and larger turkey dishes that he had always wanted to make. A few years before, he had been asked by a friend who was a fisherman to produce long, flat dishes on which to serve sides of smoked salmon. David had made a few slab-rolled pieces cut out in the shape of a salmon and painted with the fish's distinctive markings. But they had been time-consuming to produce and the loss-rate in firing had been high. George Dear had a manual extruder with which he had made umbrella stands, and he agreed to lend it to Highland Stoneware. It was an eight-inch diameter metal tube with a plunger and a very long lever that two people could pull on. It represented the sort of

unsophisticated technology that David had always liked, and it produced what was required. Long extrusions were squeezed from it, shaped rather like guttering pipes; the end naturally twisted as it came out of the machine, just like the flowing movement of a fish's tail. The nose was shaped by hand. The long, shallow dishes were decorated with salmon or other fish, making them not only practical pieces of tableware, but objects of striking beauty to be displayed when not in use.

Over 2,500 fish dishes were made on the manual extruder in little over a year before it was replaced·with a hydraulic machine designed and made locally. Graham Anderson, who runs a light engineering workshop in Lochinver, modelled the device on a matchbox which he cut up to visualise how the extruder would operate. This sort of local research and development has always been important to Highland Stoneware, a firm situated in an area remote from the kind of specialist support services on which manufacturing industry usually relies. The hydraulic extruder cost less than £1,000 to develop and build, and it has made a disproportionately large contribution to the company's commercial success.

David, Linda and Paul had painted fish on some special pieces for exhibitions during the 1970s, and the motif had been used on a limited amount of tableware in the 1980s. But generally a more or less schematic treatment had been used because it had proved uneconomical to paint detailed fins, tails and markings on standard items. The extruded fish dish, with its individual shape and large size, was a more prestigious piece; elaborate decoration further enhanced its value and the Highland Stoneware artists enjoyed the challenge of trying to capture the silky texture and richly glowing colours of salmon or more exotic fish. In February 1987 the dishes were shown at a trade fair in the Javitts Center,

The beginning: Grahame Clarke and a graphic artist make final adjustments to the Highland Stoneware brochure at a Harringay pub in 1985.

The end: Wet and battered cartons full of brochures arrive at Lochinver; they had been salvaged from a lorry which came off the road on the journey from Inverness.

Ducks and other birds, painted between 1985 and 1990. The goose (upper left) is the work of Liz Hoey, the grouse was painted by Dorell Pirie, and the rest are by Linda MacLeod.

Trials painted by David Grant to gauge the effects of juxtaposing colours, and of applying one colour over another. They were made in connection with the early development of the *Quilt* pattern.

New York; they made a vivid splash of colour which attracted a huge amount of attention – and orders. Hundreds of them were sold; altogether the firm took orders worth $45,000 at the fair.

The Kasuga company were eager to market the fish dish in Japan and sold hundreds over the next few years. The firm had first bought Highland Stoneware at a trade fair held in the Scottish Exhibition and Conference Centre, Glasgow, in February 1986. Tom Nagai, the buyer, had been attracted by a smart new brochure which Grahame Clarke had put together in London. Good colour photographs showing the wares to advantage and reproduced against a wash drawing by Grahame of Suilven and the coast at Lochinver made an eye-catching format which would be used by the company for almost ten years. In 1987, Kasuga placed a very substantial repeat order. Curiously, they preferred the more schematic fish drawing and asked for this to be continued on their fish dishes. Another pattern of which Kasuga ordered huge quantities was *Sheep NM*, tableware painted with the *Sheep* pattern bounded by a blue line. It was not the most interesting of the patterns to paint, and when Dorell Pirie, one of the decorators, was given yet another large batch to do, she commented sadly: 'Forever and ever, NM.'

Dorell was one of the several new decorating artists needed by Highland Stoneware as the number of patterns multiplied and output increased. Linda had followed *Hens* with *Ducks* and then *Frogs*, all leading eccentric lives and following atypical pursuits. She started painting *Cats* when she was inspired by her own, Florence. They, too, were soon behaving oddly, and, when they weren't dreaming of fish, might be seen in almost any non-feline role. Janey Heap-O'Neill started decorating in the mid-Eighties and contributed to the development of the *Birds* decoration and originated the *Quilt* pattern. The latter started off as 'Tartan', but when another company, quite

independently launched a range of tartan-decorated china at about the same time, amid a blare of publicity, she diverted her interested in fabrics into the area of patchwork quilts. For *Quilt*, she used extensively the technique of applying colours with cut sponges. In 1992, Janey would leave to live in France.

To some extent, *Quilt* had been derived from a pattern developed by David Grant, *Boats*, inspired by the fishing boats coming and going on the sea-loch seen through the factory windows. Both patterns were composed of patches of bright colours, including the red, *sang de boeuf* glaze. In 1986, David began to explore a motif which has fascinated him ever since. The writer of an article in the *Scots Magazine*, visiting the factory that year, noticed 'a collection of close-up photographs of local rock pools' in the studio. 'Great form and colours there,' David had commented. The flickering light falling on objects under the water seemed to David a phenomenon particularly appropriate to the qualities of Highland Stoneware, where the colours lie bright and clear beneath the surface of the vitrified glaze. Each piece of *Rock Pool* is an investigation into this analogy, as well as an exercise in the arrangement of shifting elements in a balanced composition.

In 1987, Rae Phipps returned to decorating. She had done a little when Highland Stoneware had first opened, but had stopped after a year; she had had children to look after. Now, they were no longer infants and Rae started again to paint pieces of pottery. At a Save the Children Fund event in 1988 she was helping one of the schoolchildren paint a plate; the child was trying to paint a puffin, quite a common bird in those parts, and Rae realised that Highland Stoneware was already using all the necessary colours. The *Puffin* decoration was born. Rae also introduced the twenty-two inch turntable so a decorator could work on more than one piece at a time, and so have to change brush less frequently.

Above: John Wood makes a bread crock using the combined jolleying and throwing method that he devised in 1989.

Right: Decorators sitting in front of the Ullapool showroom, c1990; from left, Liz Hoey, Tricia Thom and Terry Page.

The decorating area of Lochinver, c1991. From left, Janey Heap-O'Neill, Sheila Matheson, David Grant, Linda MacLeod, Carol Sinclair (an Aberdeen student on a study-visit).

David Grant was at Burberry's in Paris during the week before Christmas 1988, giving demonstrations of decorating.

Tricia Thom, a ceramics graduate from Gray's School of Art, Aberdeen, who had won a top award at an international exhibition in Munich, was recommended to David by Ian Pirie and taken on in July 1986. As well as contributing to the development of the *Fish* decoration, she introduced two new patterns, *Triangles* and *Vase of Flowers*. The latter, with its Fauvesque colouring and composition, is a *tour de force*. Alas, she stayed at Highland Stoneware only a few years. In 1987, Dorell Pirie, who had also studied at Aberdeen, joined the company. She first worked mainly on *Fish*, as well as *Sheep NM*, but she soon started painting all the other patterns. Two other Aberdeen students started with Highland Stoneware at about this time. Lesley Thorpe, who graduated in 1987, was taken on to work specifically on extruding fish dishes needed to fill the orders taken in America; she soon started to decorate them as well and made her own distinctive contribution to the pattern. John Wood joined the firm in 1988 after graduating in ceramics at Aberdeen and worked at Ullapool where he developed a technique of combining jolleying with throwing to make lamp bases, bread crocks and planters.

If developing a method of combining jolleying with throwing attests David's encouragement of technical innovation, his support for links with education is shown by the close relations which were established between Highland Stoneware and Gray's School of Art at Aberdeen. Ian Pirie, the head of the ceramics department, offered technical assistance whenever he could; as we have seen, he provided an oxygen probe analyser and later arranged for extruder profiles to be cut on the College's computer-assisted machine. Visiting groups of students

gained invaluable experience at Lochinver of teamwork and a semi-industrial technology. David lectured at Aberdeen on the latter, a subject which tends to be neglected in the ceramics curricula of most art schools. On the 12th October 1989, Professor Eric Spiller, Head of Gray's School of Art, wrote in a letter to David on some administrative matter:

'The maintenance of a close working relationship with Highland Stoneware is of particular importance to this School, and the opportunities that you provide for our students are valued.'

David has lectured at other art colleges, including the Royal College of Art and the Edinburgh, Cardiff and Glasgow Schools of Art. Students from several art schools have visited Lochinver on work placements.

While maintaining links with educational institutions, it has always been David's concern to give Highland Stoneware itself an educational role. Decorators have travelled to stockists and trade shows, giving them the opportunity not only to learn what the public are buying, but to see their own work in the perspective of what is currently being produced worldwide. Often these trips have been combined with visits to museums and exhibitions which enable staff to gain an historical perspective. For instance, in February 1988, Linda and Dorell spent a day at the International Spring Fair in the National Exhibition Centre, Birmingham, meeting buyers on the Highland Stoneware stand and looking at other firm's products; they then went on to London where they visited Liberty's, the Craftsman Potter's Shop, Harrod's, and other shops selling decorated pottery, as well as the British Museum and the Victoria & Albert Museum. In 1987, this policy of continuously widening the horizons of the workforce and of sending members of staff on courses to improve their skills and acquire new ones, as well as organising training for individuals within the factory, won Highland Stoneware a National Training Award. (David was delighted to find Highland Stoneware at the head of a column in the list of award winners, immediately above IBM and ICI!)

The *Scotland on Sunday* of 18th March 1990, carried an article about Highland Stoneware headlined 'Fired in the furnaces of creativity'; the last paragraph read:

'He [David Grant] is impressed by the prospectus of Ross and Cromarty Enterprise which advocates a client-led approach and proclaims that training is a lifelong pursuit for all. "This is how we see people. We want them to work to develop themselves. People want to work here, they like the creative element involved. We want to keep the energy coming through in the work and showing in each piece."'

David might well have been feeling that at least some of his aims and ideals, first articulated when he had been a student at the Royal College of Art seventeen years before, had been achieved.

CHAPTER 5

STAMINA

Staff gather at the door of the 90 cubic feet kiln to celebrate its 500th firing. From left, David Grant, Jennifer Grant, Eleanor Yates, Alison McGowan, Lorna Jones, Duncan Campbell, two hiding, Ruth Goldie, Alexa Grant, Dorell Pirie and Lesley Thorpe behind Alexa, Rae Phipps.

In 1990 the 90 cubic feet kiln at Lochinver was fired for the 500th time, seven years after it had been installed. Due to the dramatic increase in production made since 1983, the next 500 would be achieved in only another three years. During that period there would be a serious recession which was to affect almost all of British industry, but Highland Stoneware would survive unscathed. How?

One very important reason was the efficient business systems that had been introduced during the second half of the 1980s. Sandy Wemyss, of the Highlands and Islands Development Board management unit, had devised systems which were simple to run yet ideally suited to the complex and variable nature of Highland Stoneware's product range. Norah Grant, David's wife, had taken over running the office from Elizabeth Templeton in 1983, and she appreciated the method and organisation that Sandy

had introduced. She could now single-handedly manage the flow of materials, orders and stock as well as dealing with the paperwork involved in employing over twenty people. In 1988 the office was computerised and she quickly assimilated the new technology. Some have wondered why Norah, a graduate in painting and drawing, has always refused to decorate a single piece of pottery, but the efficiency of the Highland Stoneware office is at least some compensation for the loss.

The firm's efficient administration was recognised when Highland Stoneware won the Highland Small Business Award in 1987, which was followed three years later, when turnover had passed the £1/4 million mark, by the full Highland Business Award. One important aspect of the well-organised system which Norah now ran was that it enabled her to keep in regular contact with clients. Clearly,

Three men in a boat. Stuart Grant (furthest from the camera), and David Queensberry leave Eduardo Paolozzi to do the work, Lochinver, 1992.

close relationships with major customers are particularly important in a recession, and Highland Stoneware benefited enormously during the lean years from having an ever-variable, ever-growing range of decoration. Many retailers had discovered that their customers actually preferred the differences in the painting of a pattern from piece to piece, in itself a minor revolution in the tableware trade. For over a hundred years, identical decoration on every piece of each pattern had been a rule that manufacturers had disregarded at their peril.

The decorators enjoy the freedom to improvise and innovate that Highland Stoneware not only allows but encourages. On the eve of one trade show in the late 1980s, Rae Phipps decided to paint a red dog-rose instead of a blue one, on a piece of *Elphin*. She was encouraged to do so by the better reds that had been coming from the improved kiln. Away went the red dog-rose to the trade fair and at the end of the opening day David rang up to report on business:

Plate painted by Rae Phipps, c1988, which went to a trade show as a dog-rose and came back as *Poppy*!

Julian Smith threw pots for Highland Stoneware at Ullapool on a contract basis while running his own, independent pottery.

'Tell Rae they loved the poppy; they've ordered masses of it!' Thus are new patterns created! More seriously, that sort of flexibility is invaluable during a recession.

Dorell Pirie created a variation of *Poppy* when she developed the Icelandic poppy decoration, known as *Dorell Blue*. She had seen a particularly intense, deep blue on a piece painted by one of the other decorators who, however, had been unable to recall how it had been achieved. Dorell, through intelligent deduction as much as by trial and error, managed to recreate the tone. In 1991, the *Iris* decoration was first painted by Rae Phipps who had been inspired by a Hokusai print that she had seen in an exhibition at the Royal Academy. She had been in London giving a demonstration at Harrod's, and the creation of the new pattern is a good illustration of how a policy of encouraging decorators to be aware of current trends and historical examples can prove productive. David, meanwhile, was being inspired in a more relaxed way. Now and then, he managed to sneak a day's fishing and in the intervals between trout he intensely observed the clear waters of loch or burn. He utilized this visual experience in developing his *Rock Pool* decoration. In 1992, the first orders were placed, and the new pattern was

Group of trial pieces in the *Poppy* pattern. They were all painted by Rae Phipps, c1989, and show various levels of success achieved with the difficult *sang de boeuf* colour.

shown at the Aviemore trade show at the end of October. It was useful to be able to introduce such an innovative design in the depth of a recession; one could not always rely on the sort of lucky chance which had occurred earlier that year. An Italian had wandered into the showroom at Lochinver and had bought 120 dinner services plus cakestands and large spaghetti bowls – £7,000 of tableware – for a new hotel near Milan!

New patterns often result from new colours being added to the palette and new colours are sometimes devised in response to the decorators' demands. This two-way creative flow intensified during the early 1990s when Lesley Thorpe spent some time on colour development work. She conferred on the telephone with Grahame Clarke who had built up the Highland Stoneware palette with a wide range of pigments compatible with the glazes used. The more consistent results from the improved kiln assisted her, and so did Alexa Grant, now in her sixth year at school, who worked on the pigments, for a chemistry project. Lesley introduced some green tones, including the Kirsty green which fires green when applied thick and purple when thin. She also produced a new yellow pigment by modifying Grahame's original formula. Alexa devised a new green and a new blue, known appropriately as 'Alexa Green' and 'Alexa Blue'. Work on the colours was intermittent, much of it done during January when the pottery was less busy.

Two patterns which exploited the new colours were *Wild Berry* and *Pansy*. Tracey Montgomery, who developed *Wild Berry*, joined Highland Stoneware in 1992 having graduated from Aberdeen two years earlier. The visual intricacy of brambles had always attracted her, but the immediate inspiration for the new pattern was a page bordered with a design of berries that she had come across in a magazine. On tableware, *Wild Berry* is generally painted round the rims of pieces such as plates and bowls. The leaves are applied with a cut-out sponge and the berries are painted with a brush; the new purple and green are used as well as the red *sang de boeuf*. Some customers commented that the effect was rather autumnal, so Tracey

Large jug thrown by Julian Smith and painted in coloured glazes by Lesley Thorpe, c1996.

The twenty-two inch turntable was introduced by Rae Phipps to allow decorators to paint more than one piece at a time, so having to change brush less frequently. Here, Tracey Montgomery is decorating four cheese dishes simultaneously with *Spring Flowers*: the sponges lying in the saucers of pigment are cut in the shape of the leaves in the pattern.

David Queensberry has visited Lochinver most years since Highland Stoneware was started. Here he watches David Grant decorating a bowl in the upstairs studio in 1994.

devised the *Spring Flowers* pattern which also makes extensive use of cut sponges and features the new yellow on the primroses. *Pansy* was developed by Rae Phipps. It had been tried some years earlier with only limited success but now Rae saw an illustration of pansies in Kaffe Fassett's book *Glorious Inspirations* and realised that the expanded palette included most of the colours required.

The continual appearance of new patterns on the Highland Stoneware stand at trade shows throughout the recession kept the company's order-books full. In October 1992, David Grant told a reporter from the Inverness paper *Press and Journal*:

'Exports have throttled back but our sales are still ahead of production and we have plenty of orders in hand... These may be bad times for consumer spending, but we are convinced there is still an opportunity in the market for manufacturing something of sufficient quality and imagination.'

The following year, although space had been reserved at the Top Drawer trade fair in London, David decided not to attend as there were already enough orders to keep the company in full production for some time to come (and he managed to get his deposit refunded). As well as new patterns, new products were frequently introduced. John Wood's combined jolleying and throwing technique had inaugurated a range of several different lamp bases. The number of items made with the extruder had grown; three sizes of fish server (the largest one nearly three-feet long), rectangular turkey dishes up to two-feet long, plant troughs, tiles and cornices. The turkey dishes were decorated with the eponymous bird, its tail feathers displayed, usually painted by Linda MacLeod, Lesley Thorpe or Dorell Pirie; their manufacture involved pressing the extruded clay in a mould. The extrusion process itself seemed to align the clay particles in such a

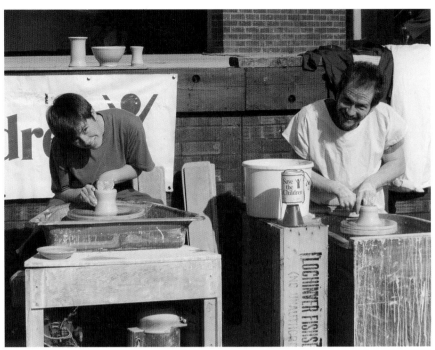

The extension to the harbour at Lochinver was officially opened in 1992. At the ceremony Audrey Paton and John Wood showed children how to throw and invited them to try their hand in aid of the Save the Children Fund.

Ruth Goldie aligning a length of extruded cornicing for a tile panel frame, 1996.

way that these very large pieces could be successfully fired without warping or buckling. Tiles were used for signs outside the potteries in Ullapool and Lochinver, and some fireplaces and kitchen walls were tiled as special commissions. Tile panels would come later.

The extruder had soon become Ruth Goldie's area of expertise. Ruth had started working for Highland Stoneware in 1988 and had helped to operate the original extruder for two months before the hydraulic version had been installed. She had developed the technique of forming the fish dishes, and she worked on the shapes of other extruded items. In her spare time, she studied at the

Open College of Art, painting and drawing at home and attending tutorials in Inverness. She gained a certificate and began to do some decorating. Working with her on some of the shapes produced by the extruder was Audrey Paton, an Aberdeen student who had worked for Highland Stoneware on student placements during the summers of 1989 and 1990 before joining the staff full-time when she had graduated the following year. She made the moulds for the large extruded dishes. Audrey has mostly worked as a decorator but during her student placements she helped develop a range of porcelain jewellery. Small pieces of jewellery made excellent kiln fillers and she modelled some

Porcelain bowls and 10ins (25.5cms) cakestand painted by Linda MacLeod with designs in cobalt nitrate (flow blue) under a clear glaze, 1990.

Driving north from Ullapool, the traveller is seduced by a big tiled sign which stands at the entrance to the pottery.

brooches in the form of fish as well as some exquisite earrings in the form of tiny seashells. Grahame Clarke had worked with Nigel Wood at the Royal College of Art in 1987 to produce a porcelain body which would be compatible with the Highland Stoneware glazes and colours. Around 1990, a number of trial pieces were fired, and in the following years Tracey Montgomery did some research into casting porcelain shapes.

On his fiftieth birthday Gordon Kilgour was presented with a cake specially iced with appropriate decoration by Audrey Paton.

In 1993, local newspapers greeted the announcement of the 1,000th firing of the kiln at Lochinver with headlines such as 'All fired up over sales successes', and 'Firing on all cylinders'. The worst of the recession was over and Highland Stoneware had not merely survived but was flourishing. The company now produced between 60,000 and 80,000 pieces of pottery a year and the workforce had grown too large for the Christmas party to be held in the Grants' home. Some of the plant was creaking, even if (most of) the staff were young and vibrant. In July 1994, one of the bisque kilns at Lochinver, a veteran of '75, was replaced, and in 1995 Robert Hudson and Alan Pett, who run the Tain Pottery, were installing a sliphouse and filter press to replace the mixing machines. At the end of June, David and Norah set off for a three-week holiday in Canada. They needed the break.

CHAPTER 6

CELEBRATIONS

Not long after his return from Canada, David was honoured to serve as Chieftain at the Assynt Games in Lochinver. The post is approximately analogous to that of Lord of Misrule at a medieval carnival, but perhaps a little more formal. The Chieftain is given a crook, an emblem of his or her authority, and has to make a speech. In his, David recalled the advent of Highland Stoneware to the village. 'It is now over twenty years since we first came to Lochinver to establish the pottery,' he said, and he remembered one of the villagers, Johnny Macrae, well-known to his audience, visiting the factory soon after it had been opened. He had looked round the building for some time, and then he had turned to David and said: 'My! This would make a grand restaurant. What Lochinver really needs is a restaurant. Do you think you will make a go of this pottery?'

In 1995, the success of Highland Stoneware was irrefutable. The firm's products might be found in kitchens and dining rooms all over the world. Vases, bowls and table lamps graced homes in Britain, Europe, America and Asia. Annual turnover was more than £1/2 million, and between twenty-five and thirty people had full-time jobs at Lochinver and Ullapool. Since then, the pace of technical innovation and artistic creativity has scarcely slackened, but time has been found to celebrate the firm's twenty-first anniversary, and to ponder a moment the direction that should be taken in the future.

If it seems odd that a company enjoying its twenty-fifth anniversary in 1999 should have been celebrating its twenty-first only three years earlier, it can be explained quite easily. The year 1996 saw the twenty-first anniversary of the factory opening in Lochinver; 1999 is the twenty-fifth anniversary of the company's establishment in 1974. Besides, the year 2000 is already scheduled for quite enough celebrations of one sort or another!

The main event of the twenty-first anniversary was to be an exhibition at John Donald's, the oldest china shop in Edinburgh, during the Festival in August. The makers and decorators would all put a lot of effort into producing an impressive collection of special pieces, but first there was somebody else's twenty-first anniversary to help celebrate. Louis Mulcahey's pottery near Ballyferriter on the Dingle peninsula had been established in 1974 and was a similar size to Highland Stoneware. David Grant had been there on a trip to Eire in 1992 and now Mulcahey invited him to come over and to bring some of the Highland Stoneware staff with him. Julian Smith, an independent potter who threw part-time at Ullapool, Alison McGowan (maker), Colette Thompson (extruder), Ruth Goldie and Lesley Thorpe went with David and Norah to share in the festivities. There were potters from many parts sharing knowledge and demonstrating techniques. The climax was a party in the style which only the Irish know how to achieve. The girls from Highland Stoneware were persuaded to sing and their performance as the Mayhem Sisters rocketed them to instant international stardom!

A group of Highland Stoneware staff went to Louis Muhcahey's pottery on the Dingle peninsula in Ireland to help celebrate its 21st anniversary in 1996. From left, Lesley Thorpe, Norah Grant, Ruth Goldie, Julian Smith, Colette Thompson, David Grant, Alison McGowan.

Celebrations reach their climax at the 21st anniversary party, July 1996. Highland Stoneware staff give it their all: from left, Duncan Campbell, Lesley Thorpe, Muriel Standlick, Julian Smith, Jean Cossar, Tracey Montgomery, Norah Grant, Rae Phipps (behind), Audrey Paton, Gordon Kilgour, Bethanie Lewis, Paul Phipps (behind), David Grant, Donna Mackenzie, Alison McGowan, John Wood, Ruth Goldie, Pippa Peacock, Fiona Mackay, Linda MacLeod.

Back in Lochinver and Ullapool the pressure was on to make and decorate pieces for the Edinburgh exhibition as well as to fill orders and keep the two factory shops stocked. On the 13th July, an open day was held at the Lochinver factory to give people from the village a preview of some of the exhibition, and to paint a piece of pottery themselves if they wanted to. In the evening, there was a big party in the village hall, and, once again, most of the staff seem to have burst into song.

The exhibition at the John Donald shop in Bristo Place, Edinburgh, started on the 1st August and stayed open through the whole month. Julian Smith had thrown

Graham Anderson, seen here at the factory open day held in July 1996. He has often helped out Highland Stoneware with running repairs to the firm's equipment and in 1987 he built the hydraulic extruder which greatly enhanced the pottery's production capacity.

The original Highland Stoneware team at the 21st anniversary party held in the village hall at Lochinver. From left, Rae Phipps, Gordon Kilgour, Norah Grant, David Grant, Paul Phipps, Linda MacLeod.

Windows full of Highland Stoneware during the 21st Anniversary Exhibition at John Donald & Co. in Edinburgh, August 1996.

some pieces, and Alan Pett others, including several large ones, a new development in the use of the Highland Stoneware clay. Among the exhibits were examples of new and revived patterns. Tracey Montgomery showed pieces decorated with apples and lemons, a stage in the development of the *Fruit* pattern. *Cockerels*, painted by Linda, were a revival of the earlier *Hens*, though these birds were much stronger images derived from Oriental art. Rae Phipps contributed some pieces decorated with *Sunflowers*, a recently introduced pattern, and others with *Poppy*. There had been much experimental work done with the *sang de boeuf*, and the colour was improving in depth and intensity all the time. A large flared bowl painted with vines bearing clusters of grapes was offered by Ruth Goldie, and Lesley Thorpe presented a big tile panel showing fish which has since been installed in Alaska.

Some *Landscape* and *Seascape* pieces in the exhibition would have interested anybody familiar with earlier examples of the patterns. David Grant had been impressed by the work of the Scottish Colourists that he had seen reproduced in recently published books. He had been intrigued by the way that Cadell and Peploe in particular had treated the Scottish landscape, and he had noticed that some of the strong colours that they had used were available on the Highland Stoneware palette. He succeeded in emulating particular effects on some *Seascape* decoration that he was doing, and he passed on his discovery to one of the more recently arrived decorators who had made a speciality of the *Landscape* pattern. Pippa Peacock had joined Highland Stoneware in 1993. She loved walking and climbing in the hills and quickly started painting the *Landscape* pattern, to which she has made her own personal contribution. At first, she used photographs that she had taken on her walks for source material. Then David steered her towards the paintings of the Scottish Colourists, and elements of their work began to show in her decoration. Patches of bright red, for example, purple mountains whose forms are explained only in terms of colour and contour, and a flattened perspective, are stylistic effects that link her *Landscapes* to their canvasses.

In May 1997, David and Norah made a trip to London – their first, they were shocked to realise, for four years. But within a few months they were back again, this time so that David could pick up the MBE that he had been awarded in the Birthday Honours list.

There have been three recent developments which have added to the Highland Stoneware repertoire – dark backgrounds, tile panels and porcelain. Since the early 1980s, the only ground glaze used by the firm had been the HS4OTT, which has the soft grey tone so hospitable to the palette used at the pottery until some more intense

The proprietors of John Donald & Co., Mr and Mrs Thomson, tidy their Edinburgh shop before the opening of the Highland Stoneware 21st Anniversary Exhibition, held during the Edinburgh Festival, August 1996.

Bill Harvey had often arranged displays of Highland Stoneware round the world during his time as a commercial manager for Highland Craftpoint. In 1996, he came out of retirement and helped set up the 21st Anniversary Exhibition in Edinburgh.

Alan Pett threw many of the large vases which were specially made for the 21st Anniversary Exhibition of Highland Stoneware.

Right: Tracey Montgomery shaping an extruded plant trough, 1994.

Far right: In 1997, an open day was held at Highland Stoneware's Ullapool pottery, and among the guests was George Dear, seen here keeping his hand in at the wheel. As a crafts adviser with Highland Craftpoint, George had helped the company with many technical problems.

colours started appearing. They, however, have induced almost a stained-glass aesthetic to some of the decoration. Inspired by what she had learnt and seen on the trip to Ireland, Lesley Thorpe began to work on glazes and developed a succession of coloured ones, including a blue. originally created by Grahame Clarke, which is now extensively used. Two patterns have been painted on the dark ground with different colours to those used for the decoration on the lighter ground. Fiona Mackay, who joined Highland Stoneware in 1996 after graduating at Aberdeen, has developed both of them – *Dark Sheep* and *Dark Landscape*. Lesley Thorpe's work has also helped to promote the use of *sang de boeuf* as a glaze as well as a colour, and some of the painted decoration on this ground has been strikingly beautiful.

The second recent development has been the painting of tile panels. This statement is not quite accurate, because the first tile panel was painted at Highland Stoneware as long ago as 1980. But the advent of the extruder has made the manufacture of tiles much more straightforward, and whenever panels have been exhibited they have sold readily and often lead to further commissions. Most of the firm's artists paint panels, sometimes two of them collaborating on a single panel. For instance, Tracey might

Kaffe Fassett (centre) recently visited Lochinver, and his energy and imagination, as well as his designs were an inspiration to the Highland Stoneware decorators. Here he is seen with Rae Phipps (left) and Brandon Mably.

do the plants on a panel, and Dorell would do the animals; or Audrey might do some flowers and an otter in the foreground of a landscape painted by Pippa.

The making of porcelain has long been one of David Grant's cherished ambitions. As we have seen, a porcelain body compatible with the firm's colours and glazes was devised by Grahame Clarke and Nigel Wood towards the end of the 1980s. Tracey Montgomery's work on porcelain shapes during the early 1990s had to be curtailed because there were orders which needed filling. But fresh impetus came to the project in 1998 when David Grant visited China. He saw the principal collections of Chinese ceramics in Beijing and Shanghai and his longstanding admiration for Oriental porcelain was refuelled. On his return to Lochinver he had the latest and youngest employee Niall Robertson, prepare a ton-and-a-half of the porcelain clay, and Steve Paterson and Paul Gow, both throwers working at Ullapool, began accustoming themselves to its characteristics. Porcelain made by Highland Stoneware has been bought by a restaurant just outside Lochinver, The Albannach, whose place-settings now have porcelain plates standing on large stoneware dishes decorated with the *Rock Pool* pattern. A Chinese emperor would be happy to eat off them!

The slogan which appears on the firm's latest brochure, 'Art Pottery – Designed to be used', denotes a new direction in Highland Stoneware's policy. The original intention was to make tableware with the ceramic qualities of studio-pottery, and the manufacture of practical ware is likely to remain a major activity of the company. But the artistic merit of Highland Stoneware has been so refined and developed that the product has outstripped much of the studio-pottery made in Britain

today in terms of ceramic quality. Collectors have begun to buy individual pieces specially decorated for exhibitions, and probably more of these will be made in the future. It has been widely recognised that the policy of allowing the decorators ample freedom of expression encourages the variation and innovation that collectors enjoy, and David Grant has recently been trying to introduce more creative freedom into the making as well as the decorating of Highland Stoneware, putting more emphasis on throwing. David also believes in the role that visiting artists can play in the generation of new ideas. The potters Archie McCall and Richard Dewar, and the sculptor Sir Eduardo Paolozzi have visited over the last few years and recently the artist and craftsman Eric Marwick, David's friend from art college days, stayed at Lochinver and decorated some porcelain pieces. Earlier this year, Sally Tuffin the fashion and ceramic designer visited the pottery and painted some vases in her distinctive style. More recently, Kaffe Fassett, the knitwear designer, spent a weekend at Highland Stoneware and his visit generated a highly creative energy. The very presence of artists of such calibre is a stimulation to all who work there, and it is David's hope that such encounters will lead to ever greater pots.

INDEX TO THE ILLUSTRATIONS

Pattern names are italicised.

The Lochinver showroom, 1999.

VARIED FLORAL   BLUE FLORAL

Until recently, floral patterns were sold as *Varied Floral*. Now, they are known by their individual pattern names.

Above, *Varied Floral* pattern trials by David Grant, c1983.

Right, *Varied Floral* patterns by David Grant with different methods of wax resist decoration, left to right, latex c1988, hot wax c1980, brushed wax in pigment c1983.

Below left, a geranium design by David Grant, in production c1982.

Below right, foxgloves by David Grant, centre and right with the Lochinver glaze, plate 12ins (30.5cms), in production c1981.

Bottom left, left and centre by Terry Page, centre and right sold as *Blue Floral* c1992.

Bottom right, *Blue Floral*, iris by Terry Page c1990.

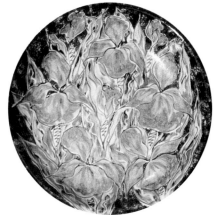

Top, *Varied Floral,* from left, decorated by Lesley Thorpe, Tracey Montgomery, Sheila Matheson, Rae Phipps, Sheila Matheson, in production c1993. This colour development led to the *Spring Flowers* range.
Above left, Icelandic poppies, an early version of *Dorell Blue,* in production c1993.
Above, *White Floral* development by Linda MacLeod, ashet 18ins (46.5cms), c1992.
Left, *Christmas Roses* sold by Liberty's of London, designed by Liz Hoey and Terry Page in Ullapool, c1992.
Bottom, *White Floral* developed by Linda MacLeod and *Dorell Blue* by Dorell Pirie, introduced c1992 and still in production.

LILY

Top, *Lily* by Dorell Pirie, first sold as *Varied Floral*, c1992.

Left, *Lily* by Dorell Pirie, 17ins (43cms), c1992.

Below, *Lily* from the current range, decorated by Dorell Pirie. The lily has been painted on a dark background since 1995.

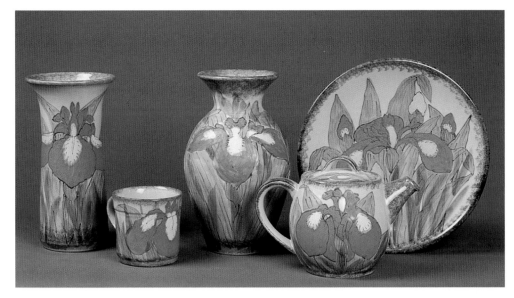

Left, *Iris* was developed by Rae Phipps in 1991 and inspired by a Hokusai print. A selection from the current range.

Above, nesting bowls, c1994.

Bread crocks: left, the pale blue 'Alexa Blue' developed by Alexa Grant as a sixth-year chemistry project. The crock on the right decorated by Audrey Paton on a blue glaze, 1998.

An early oval dish decorated by Rae Phipps, with a sponged border, 1992.

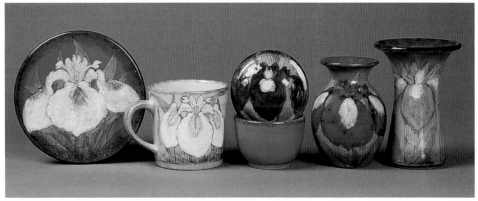

A selection of the current range showing the different colourways on giftware and tableware.

A selection of the *Poppy* pattern developed by Rae Phipps, from the current range of giftware and tableware.

Left, early development of the *Poppy* pattern by Rae Phipps, 1989. **Right,** a *Poppy* ashet showing the colour changes to the red flowers dependent on the atmosphere and heat of the kiln in the reduction firing.

Early development of the *Sunflower*, by Rae Phipps, 10ins (25.5cms), 1994.

A selection of the *Sunflower* pattern from the current range painted on a dark background, introduced in 1997.

Top, a selection of the current range of *Anemone* developed by Tracey Montgomery, painted on giftware and tableware, introduced in 1996. (A new border was introduced in 1999.)

Above left, a selection of the current range of *Tulip* (tulips were previously painted for *Varied Floral*), introduced by Linda MacLeod in 1998.

Above right, a *Tulip* dish decorated by Linda MacLeod, 1998.

Right, *Sweet Pea* developed by Tracey Montgomery in 1993 and in production until 1997.

Bottom, *Spring Flowers*, bluebells, primroses and snowdrops, developed by Tracey Montgomery in 1995 and in current production.

PANSY   WILD BERRY

A selection of the current *Pansy* range, introduced in 1996 by Rae Phipps, influenced by Kaffe Fassett's book, *Glorious Inspirations*.

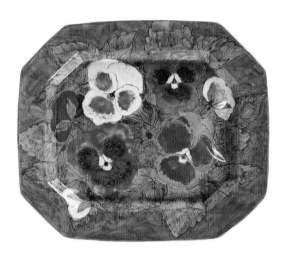

Far left, *Pansy* octagonal ashet, 16ins (40.5cms), 1998.

Left, *Wild Berry* designed by Tracey Montgomery. This bowl, hot from the kiln, was taken to the Birmingham trade fair in 1994. The reception was overwhelming and a wide range was soon developed.

A selection of the current range of *Wild Berry*. This pattern is painted on giftware and tableware.

Snowdrop developed by Linda MacLeod and introduced c1990 as *Varied Floral*. First sold as *Snowdrop* in 1999.

A selection of the current range of *Fruit* pattern, developed by Tracey Montgomery in 1996.

Strawberry, a short-lived pattern, introduced by Linda MacLeod in 1996 and in production until 1997.

'Sweet Woods', from a poem by Sir Philip Sidney, a 10ins (25.5cms), vase with *Bluebells*, made in 1999 for B. & W. Thornton of Stratford-upon-Avon in a limited edition of 50; they were thrown by Steve Paterson, and decorated by Tracey Montgomery.

Left and **above,** *Water Lily* developed by Rae Phipps after a visit to Monet's garden at Giverny. Vase, 12ins (30.5cms), 1999.

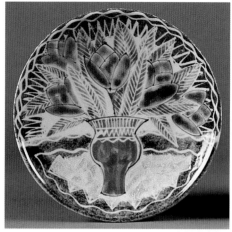
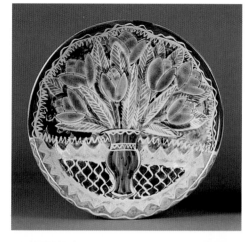

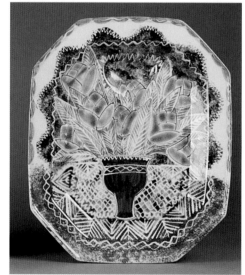

Vase of Flowers, a series of individual dishes designed and decorated by Tricia Thom, a design in the seventeenth-century English Delft tradition, 1988.

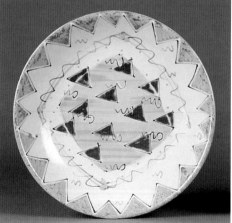

Above, *Triangles*, a sponged pattern by Tricia Thom, in production 1987.

Left, early development of the *Vase of Flowers* pattern by Tricia Thom, dish 10$^1/_2$ins (26.5cms), 1987.

Quilt, first version, pattern developed by Janey Heap-O'Neill, from 1989.

Far left and **left,** turkey dish and ashet decorated with the first version of *Quilt*, 1990.

Left, a turkey dish decorated with the *Quilt* pattern 18$^1/_2$ins (47.5cms), painted by Janey Heap-O'Neill, 1992.
Above, an interwoven design inspired by the drawings of M.C. Escher, painted by Janey Heap-O'Neill, in production c1992, part of the *Quilt* range.

Quilt, second version. A selection of the range developed by Janey Heap-O'Neill, in production 1991-92.

A turkey dish decorated by Lesley Thorpe, 18^1/$_2$ins (47.5cms), 1994.

Cockerel, a revival of *Hens* by Linda MacLeod, decorated on larger forms in Linda's distinctive current style, large jug, 13½ins (34.5cms), 1996.

Cockerel dish decorated by Linda MacLeod, 1998, showing the increased colour range developed since the 1980s.

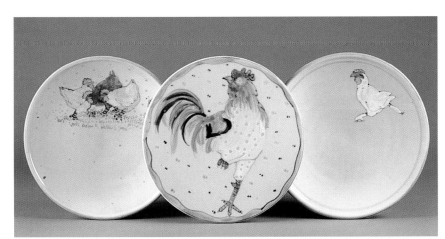

Middle, above and **right,** a selection of amusing *Hens* by Linda MacLeod in her early graphic style, c1982-88.

BIRD

Bird, usually sea birds and waders of Scotland. From left, plate by Liz Hoey; oval dish 1989, and two plates by Linda MacLeod, c1991.

Above and **right,** *Bird* designed and decorated by Liz Hoey, drawn in a distinctive style showing an Oriental influence, in production 1992-93.

Above, *Bird*, cheese dish and cover decorated by Audrey Paton, c1995. **Above right,** *Bird*, from left, plate decorated by Lesley Thorpe and two plates by Dorell Pirie, c1994. Pattern discontinued in 1996.

BIRD BOATS

The *Bird* pattern has been revived in 1999. Mallard ducks decorated by Dorell Pirie, bread crock ht. 12¼ins (31cms).

Rectangular dish painted with a black-throated diver by Audrey Paton, 17ins (43cms) long, 1999.

Plate and ashet with herons, by Lesley Thorpe, 1999.

Boats, pattern introduced by David Grant in 1987. This publicity photograph shows the hessian bag which is used as an alternative to wooden packaging.

Frog, introduced by Linda MacLeod. **Above,** vases and 15ins (38cms), rectangular dish by Ruth Goldie, with a small mug by Maria Ewen, c1989, in production until 1990. **Right,** an example of the earliest *Frog* decorated pieces, cakestand 10ins (25.5cms), by Linda MacLeod, 1986.

Diving Duck introduced by Linda MacLeod, large plate 10ins (25.5cms), in production 1994-96.

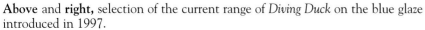
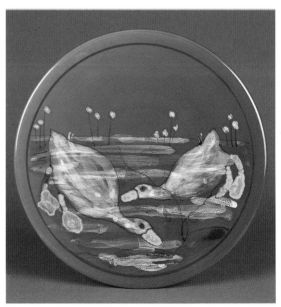

Above and **right,** selection of the current range of *Diving Duck* on the blue glaze introduced in 1997.

Left, an early *Puffin* developed by Rae Phipps and inspired by a child's plate painted for Save the Children Fund, c1988.

Above, *Puffin* ashet by Rae Phipps, 1997.

A selection of the current range of *Puffin*.

PUFFIN TILE PANEL

Puffin tile panel decorated by Rae Phipps, 1998.

SHEEP   DARK SHEEP

The development of the *Sheep* pattern introduced by David Grant in 1983. On the left, playing football, and on the right, a design inspired by Henry Moore's 'Sheep Sketchbook'.

The first *Sheep* designs by David Grant, in production 1984.

A selection from the current range of *Dark Sheep* painted on a blue-glazed ground. Developed by Fiona Mackay, 1997.

A selection from the current range of *Sheep*. (For tableware see page 83.)

Brooches modelled by Grahame Clarke, sheep and seascape painted by David Grant. In production for a short time 1992-95, and sold mainly in the Highland Stoneware showrooms.

Brooches and earrings. In 1990 Audrey Paton's first input was to model, press mould and decorate this range of jewellery.

Miniature models of crofts etc., 1982.

Miniature models of buildings in Lochinver, 1980.

Stripes, a pattern by Grahame Clarke inspired by a David Queensberry design, in production 1984.

Sponge Blue, designed by Grahame Clarke and decorated by Sheila Matheson, 1985. In production for a short time.

One of the first pieces decorated with Florence by Linda MacLeod in 1984.

A *Cat* group, decorated by Linda MacLeod in her distinctive style, teapot 6½ins (16.5cms), c1986.

A salmon dish by Linda MacLeod with a 'cat-fish', in production 1987.
Right, *Cat*, ashet decorated by Linda MacLeod c1988.

Left, middle and **right,** *Cat* dishes decorated by Dorell Pirie, c.1992.

Cat, by Dorell Pirie, c1990. The pattern was taken out of production in 1993.

Cat was revived in 1999 and is painted by the entire studio. Vase by Dorell Pirie, 12ins (30.5cms).

The clay dish in section, emerging from the extruder.

Shaping the salmon dish tail.

Cutting the tail.

Cutting the head.

Final shaping and sponging.
Right, cutting and trimming the base of the leather-hard dish.

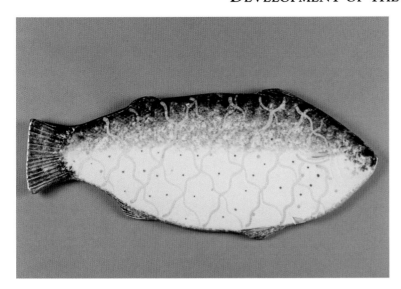

Above left, the first salmon dish designed by David Grant. A slab-rolled flat serving tray for smoked salmon, 22ins (56.5cms), 1984.

Above right, top, an early shaped dish with modelled fins by Tricia Thom for the American market, 1986; bottom, the current fish server which replaced the early version.

Right, the development of the salmon dish, decorated by (from top), Tricia Thom, 1986; Linda MacLeod, 1987; Dorell Pirie, c1992; Dorell Pirie, 1996. The longest, 30$\frac{1}{2}$ins (78cms).

Bottom left, fish server decorated by Dorell Pirie, 16ins (40.5cms), 1998.

Bottom right, the widest salmon dish in production, this example decorated by Lesley Thorpe, 25ins (64cms), 1998.

Early *Fish* designs. From left, plate decorated by Linda MacLeod, 1982; T.G. Green flan dish by Linda MacLeod, 1978; plate by Dorell Pirie, 1989; beaker by Linda MacLeod, 1979; mug by Tricia Thom, 1988.

Above left, the development of the rectangular serving dish. From top, decorated by Tricia Thom, 1988, Tricia Thom, 1992, Tracey Montgomery, 1998. Longest 18ins (46.5cms).

Above right, *Fish* ashet, designed and decorated by Tricia Thom, c1988.

Right, *Fish* plates, decorated by Dorell Pirie, 12ins (30.5cms), c1992.

Top row, from left, decorated by Audrey Paton, Dorell Pirie and Pippa Peacock, 1998.

Second row, round dish by Lesley Thorpe, oval dish by Dorell Pirie, 1998.

Third row, left, rectangular dish by Lesley Thorpe, right, one of a series of tropical fish decorated by Ruth Goldie, 1998.

Right, round dish by Pippa Peacock, ashet by Dorell Pirie, 1998.

COMMEMORATIVES

Christmas plate, 1975, by Grahame Clarke, issued in a small edition.

Left, plate commemorating a record catch by the 'Horizon', 1976; **right,** good-luck plate for the 'St. Kilda', 10ins (25.5cms), 1976. Both fishing boats belonged to John Thompson of Lossiemouth.

House, motto or name plaques were lettered by Paul Phipps, c1978.

Christmas plates, 1979 and 1977, by Linda MacLeod, 10ins (25.5cms), issued in small editions.

Above left, a Queen Elizabeth II Jubilee loving cup, designed and decorated by Grahame Clarke with sprigged plaques. Issued in a small edition, 1977.

Above right, a plate made for presentation to H.R.H. Prince Charles on the occasion of his visit to the pottery in 1979, designed and decorated by Grahame Clarke, lettering by Paul Phipps.

Left, a number of these plates were made for the Highlands and Islands Development Board; they were designed and sprigged by Grahame Clarke in 1983 and 1984.

'Spey Valley' by David Grant, a plate from a range made for the distillers Wm. Grant & Sons, Dufftown, 10ins (25.5cms), 1989.

Display plaque made for the Edinburgh retailers Jenner's, lettering by Paul Phipps, 1987. Promotional items have been made for several retailers in various designs.

Pieces made to commemorate the 500th firing of the kiln on 24th May 1990. Jug by David Grant, dish by Linda MacLeod, teapot by Ruth Goldie.

Right, a selection of pieces typical of many made for private or commercial commissions. The plate shows the Split Rock, a landmark off the Sutherland coast.

Below left, Christening set; many, in different designs have been commissioned since the early 1980s.

Below right, dish, from an edition of five made for the crew of the 'Westro'. The sea was painted by David Grant, the boat by Dorell Pirie, in 1995. 'Westro' is skippered by Graham Thompson, son of the Lossiemouth fisherman John Thompson.

Above, early lamps first introduced c1989.
Right, from left, *Lilies* by Dorell Pirie, 1998, *Tulip*
by Linda MacLeod, 1996, both in the *sang de boeuf* glaze.
Below left, *Seascape* by David Grant, 1997, and *Puffin*
by Rae Phipps, 1998.
Below right, *Cat* lamp base by Dorell Pirie, 1998 and
Landscape by Pippa Peacock, 1998.

Mirror frames introduced in 1999, made in two sizes, 13^1/$_2$ins (34.5cms) and 10^1/$_2$ins (26.5cms). *Rock Pool* decorated by David Grant,
Fish decorated by Lesley Thorpe, *Landscape* decorated by Pippa Peacock.

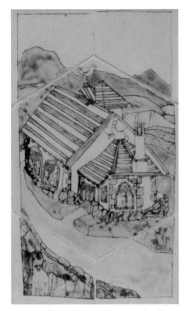

One of the first tile panels; by Linda MacLeod with the Free Church, Lochinver, c1980.

Landscape panel by Pippa Peacock, 16ins x 32ins (40.5cms x 81cms) inside frame, 1998.

Seascape panel by David Grant, 16ins x 32ins (40.5cms x 81cms) inside frame, 1998.

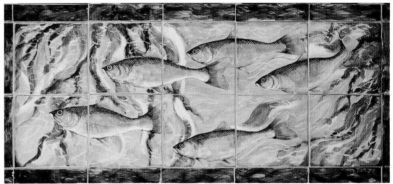

Fish panel decorated by Dorell Pirie, 16ins x 40ins (40.5cms x 102cms) inside frame, 1997.

Jungle triptych displayed in Jenner's window for the Edinburgh Festival 1997. Decorated by Dorell Pirie and Tracey Montgomery, centre panel 48ins x 32ins (123cms x 81cms) inside frame.

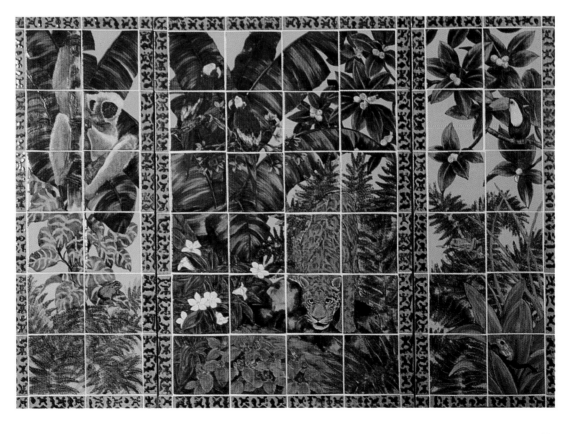

Sunflowers in a *Seascape* vase by Fiona Mackay, 24ins x 16ins (61.5cms x 40.5cms), 1998.

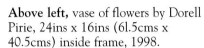

Above left, vase of flowers by Dorell Pirie, 24ins x 16ins (6l.5cms x 40.5cms) inside frame, 1998.

Above centre, Mallard ducks by Dorell Pirie, 16ins x 16ins (40.5cms x 40.5cms) inside frame, 1997.

Above right, sea birds nesting by Dorell Pirie, 32ins x 16ins (81cms x 40.5cms) inside frame, 1998.

Left, shellfish by Tracey Montgomery, 40ins x 32ins (101cms x 81cms) inside frame, 1986.

Right, fishing trawler in rough seas by Dorell Pirie, ht. 20ins x 28ins (51cms x 71.5cms) inside frame, 1996.

Below, a tiled fireplace surround by Eric Marwick, commissioned by a fishing enthusiast, 1998.

Celadon designed by David Grant, Heal's 1973.

Tableware made for the RCA degree show, 1974.

Inver, tableware designed for Conran, 1982-85.

Canisp, tableware for General Trading Company, 1983-87.

Set of *Tenmoku* nesting bowls, 1975-77.

Set of *Celadon* nesting bowls in wooden packaging, c1982.

Above, the development of *Culkein*, by Grahame Clarke, plates 8ins (20.5cms), c1981.

Left, *Culkein* tableware, 1981-1995.

Culag, (right), 1975, developed by Grahame Clarke from his version of the Immortelle pattern by Royal Copenhagen, made at the RCA, 1974.

A selection of Culag tableware, in production 1976-77.

Celadon Floral, developed by David Grant and Linda MacLeod, 1977.

Celadon Floral, an alternative version, 1978.

Elphin, developed by David Grant, c1983, in production 1981-96.

Lochinver, developed by Linda MacLeod, in production 1979-90.

Lochinver giftware, in production 1979-86.

Jig, developed by David Grant, c1983-86; on the giftware this pattern was named *Wallpaper*. From left, *Blue Jig, Jig, Jig* again, *Blue Jig, Wallpaper*.

Above, *Fishing Fly* on Lochinver glaze, originated by Grahame Clarke in 1975, in production 1981-84.

Left, *Quilt*, developed by Janey Heap-O'Neill, 1992-93, in current production with border only.

Above, *Assynt*, developed by David Grant and Linda MacLeod in collaboration with Grahame Clarke, in production 1981-88.

Left, *Fish*, developed by Dorell Pirie and Lesley Thorpe, 1993-4. Sold only in Highland Stoneware showrooms.

TABLEWARE – 1999

Top row: from left, *Traditional Floral*, *Celadon*, *Blue Edge*, *Celadon Floral*. **Second row:** from left, *Iris*, developed by Rae Phipps, *Poppy*, developed by Rae Phipps, *White Floral*, developed by Linda MacLeod. **Third row:** from left, *Landscape*, developed by Pippa Peacock, *Seascape*, developed by David Grant, *Sheep*, developed by David Grant. **Fourth row:** from left, *Wild Berry*, developed by Tracey Montgomery, *Rock Pool*, developed by David Grant, *Quilt*, developed by Janey Heap-O'Neill.

Jug and vase decorated by Linda MacLeod, the reduction red glaze particularly successful, 1996.

Lily dish by Dorell Pirie, 15ins (38cms), 1998.

Above left, *Tulip* dish by Dorell Pirie, 15¹/₂ins (39.5cms), 1995.

Above right, *Cat* bowl by Dorell Pirie, 19¹/₂ins (50cms), 1997.

Right, from left, *Fuchsia* by Audrey Paton, *Peonies* by Dorell Pirie, 12ins (30.5cms), and *Iris* by Heather Wallace, 1998.

Dish, painted with a pheasant design by Dorell Pirie, 18ins (46.5cms), 1999.

From left, floral bowl decorated by Dorell Pirie, *Tulip* jug decorated by Linda MacLeod, 9¹/₂ins (24cms), *Pansy* dish decorated by Linda MacLeod, 1997-98.

From left, bowl, decorated by Tracey Montgomery with anemones, plate and bowl decorated by Dorell Pirie with petunias, plate 10ins (25.5cms), 1998.

Vase, decorated by Lesley Thorpe with flowers, 16¹/₂ins (42cms), 1997.

Ginger jar, decorated by Ruth Goldie with rowan berries, 1999.

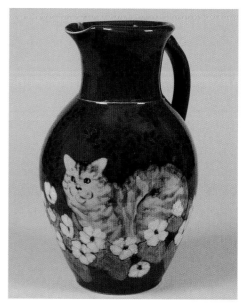

Jug, decorated by Dorell Pirie with a cat among flowers, 1998.

Rock Pool trials by David Grant, 1986-90, central plate, 1988.

A selection of the current *Rock Pool* giftware, introduced 1992.

A group of *Rock Pool* in the *sang de boeuf* glaze, small bowl, 7ins (18cms), 1999.

Above, three different colour versions of *Rock Pool*, decorated by David Grant, plates 12ins (30.5cms), in current production.

Right, porcelain plate on a *Rock Pool* stoneware under-dish, developed for restaurant use at the Albannach Hotel, Lochinver, 1999.

Specials – Etched Plates

This group of jolleyed plates, 10ins (25.5cms), was decorated by engraving the patterns into the moulds; colour slips were brushed onto the plates, which were then scraped to reveal the design and painted before glazing and firing.

Designed by Paul Phipps, shown at the Eden Court Exhibition, 1976,

Designed by David Grant, shown at the Eden Court Exhibition, 1976.

Plate by Linda MacLeod, with a design engraved directly into the clay, c1979.

From left, 'Wee Willie Winkie', 1976, and 'Flower Power', 1977, 14ins (35.5cms), both engraved by Linda MacLeod.

Above left, pair of plates jolleyed with the same engraving, but with different colouring, by Linda MacLeod.

Above right, 'Spring' and 'An Ideal Kitchen', by Linda MacLeod, 14ins (35.5cms), 1977.

Left, two plates with the Free Church, Lochinver, engraved by Linda MacLeod. The plate on the left was offered in *The Scotsman* for Christmas, 1978.

SPECIALS

One-off designs have been made at Highland Stoneware since the beginning. Freedom of expression is encouraged from all decorators, and today exciting pots are emerging from the kiln.

On the left, a design by Paul Phipps on a T.G. Green oval dish, 13ins (33cms), c1979, which led to the *Blue and White* giftware on the right, painted by Linda MacLeod, 1980.

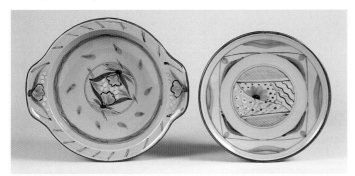 

Plates designed by Grahame Clarke, shown at the Eden Court Exhibition, 1976.

Plates designed by Grahame Clarke, c1975.

From left, honeypot, decorated by Grahame Clarke, 1976; teapot with chickens, painted by Linda MacLeod, 1999; ginger jar and lid painted with convolvulus, by Tracey Montgomery, 10ins (25.5cms), 1998.

Dish decorated by Tricia Thom, c1990.

Seascape painted by David Grant, 1998.

Dish by Lesley Thorpe, with a design influenced by Japanese art, c1995.

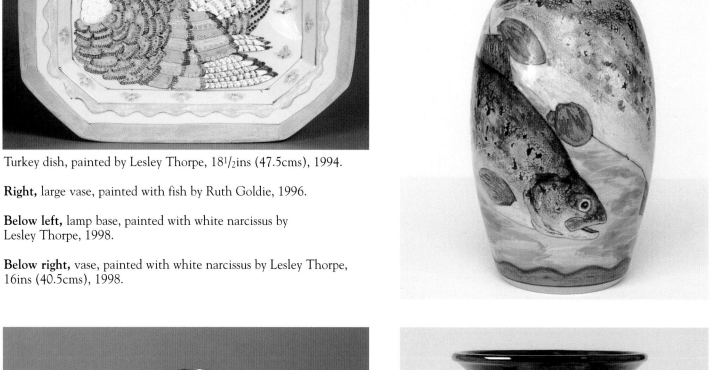

Turkey dish, painted by Lesley Thorpe, 18$^1/_2$ins (47.5cms), 1994.

Right, large vase, painted with fish by Ruth Goldie, 1996.

Below left, lamp base, painted with white narcissus by Lesley Thorpe, 1998.

Below right, vase, painted with white narcissus by Lesley Thorpe, 16ins (40.5cms), 1998.

Right, from left, vase painted with Christmas rose by Fiona Mackay, 1999; vase with oriental poppy by Heather Wallace, 16ins (40.5cms), 1999.

Far right, jug decorated with *Fish* design, by Lesley Thorpe and thrown by Julian Smith, 11¹/₂ins (29cms), 1996.

Bowl, painted with anemones by Tracey Montgomery, 16¹/₂ins (42cms), 1998.

Bowl, painted with fruit design by Tracey Montgomery and thrown by Fergus Stewart, 17¹/₂ins (45cms), 1998.

'The Owl and the Pussy Cat', dish decorated by Linda MacLeod, 15ins (38cms), 1997.

Bowl, painted with turkey inside a strawberry border, by Linda MacLeod, 1998.

A tazza from a series of blue and white rustic scenes by Lesley Thorpe, 13ins (33cms), 1998. (See pot in portrait, page 107.)

Dish, painted with a capercailzie by Dorell Pirie, wittily inscribed, 19ins (49cms), 1998.

Dish, decorated with a Skye landscape by Pippa Peacock, 18ins (46.5cms), 1998.

Dish, painted with *Puffin* by Dorell Pirie, 'The West Coast Minister', 10ins (25.5cms), c1991.

Dish, painted with an alert otter by Dorell Pirie, 19ins (49cms), 1998. Otters are often seen in Loch Inver.

LANDSCAPE

Developed by David Grant in collaboration with Grahame Clarke and Linda MacLeod from 1979.

Early *Landscape* designs by David Grant, 1979-80. Large plate, 10ins (25.5cms).

From left, plate by Linda MacLeod, 1989, beaker showing Suilven by Dorell Pirie, 1993, plate by Sheila Matheson, 1988.

Above, left, *Landscape* with trees, painted by David Grant, right, *Landscape* by Linda MacLeod, 10ins (25.5cms), c1980.

Right, *Landscape* featuring Suilven, painted by Janey Heap-O'Neill, 17ins (43cms), c1991.

Snowscape painted in the Ullapool studio, 1988-92.

Left and centre, plates decorated by Terry Page, 1993; right, plate decorated by Donna Mackenzie, 1995. Large plate, 10ins (25.5cms).

From left, plate featuring a view in Skye, 1995; plate showing Achnahaird Bay, 1993, 10ins (25.5cms); plate decorated with *Dark Landscape*, painted on the darker background, all by Pippa Peacock, 14ins (35.5cms), 1992.

A selection of *Dark Landscape*, developed by Fiona MacKay, showing the two different tones of dark blue background glaze.

LANDSCAPE

A selection from the current range.

Left, bread crock, decoration by Pippa Peacock featuring Suilven, 1998.
Above, trial sketch by David Grant, on an 8ins (20.5cms) tile, 1998.

Two views of the vase thrown by Paul Gow and decorated by David Grant and Pippa Peacock, to commemorate the 25th anniversary of the founding of Highland Stoneware. This edition of 250 vases has a special backstamp and each piece is numbered. The vase, 8¹/₂ins (21.5cms), and the mug are painted with a view of Suilven; the mug is in unlimited production during 1999, but each one is numbered.

Dish, painted by Pippa Peacock with a landscape featuring Suilven, 12ins (30.5cms), 1996.

SEASCAPE

Developed by David Grant from 1981.

Plate, 1981, and vase, 1982, both decorated by David Grant.

Seascape pieces decorated by David Grant, large plate 10ins (25.5cms), 1988.

Above, trials, painted by David Grant, showing the influence of the Scottish Colourists, c1995.

Plates by David Grant, left, featuring a view of the Split Rock, 10ins (25.5cms), c1997.

Above, bread crock and vase decorated by David Grant, 1994 and 1997.

Right, rectangular dish, decorated by Lesley Thorpe, 17ins (43cms), 1998.

A selection of *Seascape* from the current range painted by various decorators.

Tam o' Shanter, plates and mugs decorated by David Grant with scenes and quotations from Burn's poem, in production 1983-86.

Plates decorated by local children in aid of Save the Children Fund, 1985-90.

Children from the school at Stoer in Assynt with their Highland Stoneware plates, painted to raise money for the charity, 1996.

From left, plate painted by Lucy Landau when a student at Edinburgh College of Art, 1989; plate painted by an artist from the Russian porcelain company, Gzhel.

Visiting artist from the Russian porcelain company, Gzhel.

From left, plate and mug by Karen Smith; bowl made by Richard Dewar who runs his own pottery in France; and a planter painted by Sheila Notman, a visiting student of ceramics, 1986.

A selection of pieces painted by Eric Marwick, 1997-98.

Above, porcelain painted by Eric Marwick who teaches in Dundee, 1999.
Right, vase painted by fashion and pottery designer, Sally Tuffin, 1999.

The artist Eduardo Paolozzi painting a dish at Lochinver, on a visit in 1992.

Plates by Eduardo Paolozzi, left, with etched design made in collaboration with Grahame Clarke at the RCA and glazed in Lochinver, with a glaze made from Dornoch Firth stone, signed 'Eduardo Paolozzi-Grahame Clarke', 1976; right, plate painted at Lochinver, signed 'D.G. G.C. E.P.', 1976.

Plate painted by the American potter John Glick on a visit to the pottery, 1985.

Plates painted by Eduardo Paolozzi; left, signed 'E.P. G.C. D.G. at the RCA 1974'; right, signed 'E.P. Lochinver 1976', 14ins (35.5cms).

Above, left and **above,** pieces painted by Archie McCall, head of the ceramics department at Glasgow School of Art, 1989.

Vases and 8ins (20.5cms) tile, painted by knitwear designer Kaffe Fassett on a visit to Lochinver in 1999. The vase on the right is decorated with a sponged design inspired by lichens on rocks.

SUILVEN

Suilven, in her ever-changing moods and colours, dominates the Lochinver landscape. She has been a symbol to the pottery since its inception. Highland Stoneware decorators and visiting artists have always been inspired by the mountain's majestic presence.

Views of Suilven, from left, Archie McCall, Grahame Clarke, David Grant, David Grant again, and Linda MacLeod, 1978-88.

The front and back of an early leaflet showing the tableware range of shapes, 1978.

Left, front and loose leaf from a catalogue showing *Varied Floral* designs and Grahame Clarke's watercolour of Suilven. **Above,** wooden packaging displayed at a trade fair, 1982.

Undecorated Cookware shapes.

Undecorated Giftware shapes.

Undecorated Tableware shapes.

Cover and shape guide from catalogue issued in 1998, illustrated entirely by photography.

NORAH GRANT, D.A., from Dunfermline, met David in 1967 at Duncan of Jordanstone College of Art, Dundee, where she was a student of painting and drawing; they were married five years later. Since 1983 she has run the Highland Stoneware office with capability – and the diplomacy sometimes required!

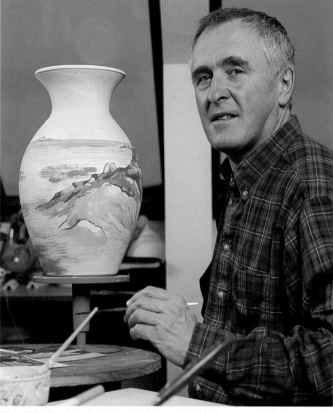

DAVID GRANT, M.B.E., M.A., (RCA), born at Achfary in the Highlands returned to his native heath to establish Highland Stoneware at Lochinver in 1975. Since then he has been not only MD, but designer, decorator, potter, chemist, engineer, salesman, educator, visionary, and a friend to all his staff.

DAVID QUEENSBERRY, F.S.I.A., started working in the ceramics industry after studying at the Central School of Art, London. His design consultancy has been responsible for some of the most innovative tableware made over the last forty years in Europe. As his professor at the RCA he recognised David's talent and vision. He is a regular visitor to Lochinver where he offers advice – in exchange for a plentiful supply of fresh seafood!

GRAHAME CLARKE, Des. RCA, studied ceramics at the RCA from 1962 to 1965 and returned there as tutor in 1970. With David Grant, one of his students, he developed the prototype of the Highland Stoneware range, and he has been responsible for most of the company's technical development, as well as contributing to its artistic success. He now also makes his own porcelain in Norfolk.

RAE PHIPPS, D.A., was a student of painting at Duncan of Jordanstone College of Art, Dundee when she met her future husband Paul. They joined Highland Stoneware at the outset, and Rae's first tasks included glaze dipping, making handles and packing. In 1987, she started decorating, and, as well as contributing several new patterns has proved an effective and amiable manager of the decorating area. She is a qualified teacher and has taught part-time in primary schools at Lochinver and Stoer.

PAUL PHIPPS, D.A., is the production manager at Highland Stoneware's Lochinver factory. He studied ceramics at Duncan of Jordanstone College of Art, Dundee, where he met David. In 1975, Paul joined David in Lochinver as soon as the factory had been built and helped get the business going. He has continued to play a vital part in the day-to-day running of the pottery, meeting every eventuality with his Yorkshire sense of humour. The local community has benefited from his interest and energy; for several years he produced the *Assynt News*.

GORDON KILGOUR is one of the longest serving members of the Highland Stoneware team. He started as a maker in March 1975. Previously he had spent three-and-a-half years working at Buchan's pottery in Portobello, near Edinburgh. He attended short training courses in Stoke-on-Trent, the first one in 1975 and another in 1983. Gordon would not like to count the number of pieces of Highland Stoneware he has jolleyed over the years not to mention quite a few he has extruded! He used to play football for the Lochinver team but hung up his boots a while ago.

LINDA MACLEOD, D.A., (née McNeill), joined Highland Stoneware in 1976, the day after she graduated in ceramics at Duncan of Jordanstone College of Art, Dundee. Her style of decoration has been an important formative influence on Highland Stoneware pottery. She has originated several patterns including *Hens, Cat, Frog* and *Duck* as well as floral designs. Linda has learnt to control a lively – sometimes surreal – imagination, although any quirkiness has usually been more of a boon than a drawback. Since 1986 she has lived in the house she and her husband built on land adjacent to the pottery.

LESLEY THORPE, B.A., first worked part-time for Highland Stoneware in 1987, taken on to help make the great number of extruded fish dishes ordered that year for the American market. Since graduating from Gray's School of Art, Aberdeen, in 1989, she has been employed full-time, mainly as a decorator. She contributed to the development of the *Fish* decoration, introducing more exotic species; they give her the opportunity to use the bright pigments she has developed in the course of her work on colour mixing. Lesley makes her own raku-fired pottery at her croft in Clachtoll, a village about five miles north of Lochinver, where she keeps horses and chickens.

TRACEY MONTGOMERY, M.A., graduated in ceramics at Gray's School of Art, Aberdeen, before gaining her MA at the Staffordshire Polytechnic. She started at Highland Stoneware in 1992, and her early work for the firm centred on the development of porcelain casting. She now makes porcelain boxes and wind-chimes in her spare time. Her contribution to the decoration of Highland Stoneware includes the *Wild Berry*, *Spring Flowers*, *Fruit* and *Anemone* patterns. She has computer skills which she uses to design the firm's promotional literature and display boards.

PIPPA PEACOCK, M.A. Vet M.B. cert V.R. M.R.C.V.S., qualified as a vet after studying at Cambridge University. She began to spend holidays in Lochinver and enjoyed walking and painting among the mountains. She decided to settle in the area and in 1993 applied to Highland Stoneware for a job. Hired as a trainee decorator, she readily transferred her painting skills from paper to pottery, and has been much involved in the development of the *Landscape* pattern. A keen climber, she is an emergency medical technician with the local Mountain Rescue team. Occasionally, in an emergency, she downs her brush to attend a sick animal!

DORELL PIRIE, (née McKinnon), was born in Australia, but spent most of her childhood in Lochinver. She studied ceramics at Gray's School of Art, Aberdeen, working during the summer vacations at Highland Stoneware. She joined the company full-time in 1987 and after working for a year on the extruder she started decorating. Dorell has displayed great skill at drawing, and her control over the Highland Stoneware palette is remarkable. *Lily* and *Dorell Blue* are patterns that she has developed herself, and she has made a significant contribution to the drawing of fish, birds, cats and wild animals. Her talents are particularly well displayed in the painting of colourful tile panels. She lives at Clachtoll, a village about five miles north of Lochinver.

AUDREY PATON, B.A. (hons), (née Whyte), first worked at Highland Stoneware on summer placements in 1989 and 1990, while a student at Gray's College of Art, Aberdeen. During this time she modelled pieces of jewellery in porcelain. She graduated in 1991 and immediately started working full-time for the pottery. Some of her time has been spent on mould-making, particularly for a lasagne dish, but usually she decorates. She likes painting on the dark blue and *sang de boeuf* glaze, and she has recently contributed divers to the new *Bird* range.

RUTH GOLDIE (née French), joined Highland Stoneware in 1988. She made an important contribution to the methods of operating the hydraulic extruder and helped to develop many of the extruded forms. Having gained a certificate in art and design at the Open College of Art, she is now taking a distance-learning course in ceramic technology at Staffordshire University. She spends half the week organising production at the Ullapool unit; at Lochinver she is involved in both making and decorating. Ruth particularly enjoys painting on the *sang de boeuf* glaze.

STEVE PATERSON, B.A., (hons), studied ceramics at Glasgow School of Art and then set up his own pottery in Dumfries. He threw for Highland Stoneware on a freelance basis in 1997 and joined the firm full-time shortly afterwards. He spent a year on production throwing, but he has since started making large pots for exhibitions as well. Last year he added decorating to his skills and is an important member of the team at Ullapool. Steve plays guitar and sings with the group Stormbound at the Ferry Boat Inn, Ullapool, a hostelry well attended by the Ullapool potters!

FIONA MACKAY, B.A. (hons), started at Highland Stoneware in 1996 after graduating in ceramics at Gray's School of Art, Aberdeen. She trained at the Lochinver factory for a year before moving to Ullapool, where she now lives and works. As well as contributing to the day-to-day running of the pottery, she does a lot of decorating and has been largely responsible for the development of *Dark Sheep* and *Dark Landscape*. Painting tile panels is a part of her job that she especially likes. In her spare time Fiona is a Brown Owl, helping to run the local Brownies.

DECORATORS

SUSAN BROWN, B.A. (hons), from Falkirk, graduated in 1997 from Salford University in visual arts and culture. She draws and paints, and at college she specialised in sculpture. She was filling in a year as an assistant at the Ceilidh Place in Ullapool when she became aware of Highland Stoneware and applied for a job. She has been at Lochinver on a course training to be a decorator, and is soon to be based at Ullapool.

HEATHER WALLACE is a qualified beauty therapist having studied at Dundee Technical College. She joined Highland Stoneware in 1997 after spending two-and-a-half years in Holland where she taught herself to draw, sketching barges and windmills. Heather works at Ullapool and decorates as well as 'doing whatever needs to be done around the pottery.'

DAWN CHAPMAN works at Lochinver as a decorator. Her years spent in retail display for large department stores have given her a sure artistic sense that she brings to the decoration of pottery. She has been at Highland Stoneware for just over a year. As a hobby she paints pictures in a folk-art style, when she can find time from running her Bed and Breakfast.

MAKERS

BUSH CAMPBELL has lived in Lochinver since he was six months old. He started working at the pottery in 1978, straight from school. His making skills were taught him by Gordon Kilgour, and now he is in the process of taking over the coordination of the making department. He was nicknamed 'Bush' for his thick, curly hair which he used to let grow long.

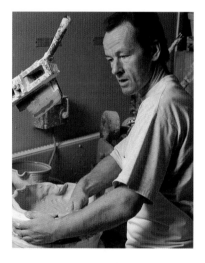

PAUL GOW, D.A., graduated from Gray's College of Art, Aberdeen, and ran his own pottery at Dingwall for a number of years, and now throws for Highland Stoneware on a contract-basis.

ALISON McGOWAN, from Hamilton, joined Highland Stoneware in 1988 and has been trained as a maker; she counts fettling, jolleying and extruding among her skills.

ANDREW McCLELLAND, born in Lochinver, left school in 1996 and shortly afterwards started at Highland Stoneware where he has proved himself a very deft glazer.

JOHN WOOD, B.A. (hons), came to Highland Stoneware as a thrower and decorator after gaining a post graduate diploma at Gray's School of Art, Aberdeen. He developed the technique of combined jolleying and throwing and until recently he managed the pottery at Ullapool. He has now left to pursue a career in show business.

Filter-pressed cakes of clay in the clay room at Lochinver.

FERGUS STEWART trained as a potter in Scotland before spending eighteen years in Australia teaching and running a succession of ceramics workshops. Over recent years he has thrown on a contract basis for Highland Stoneware.

MURIEL STANDLICK, left, joined Highland Stoneware in 1986 and works as an assembler, putting on handles, spouts and knobs. JEAN COSSAR has been with Highland Stoneware since 1982, like Muriel she works as an assembler and finisher.

JACKIE THOMA joined the firm in 1992 and is now responsible for quality control. She allocates the pots to the shop, stockroom and trade orders before packing and despatching.

From left, NIALL ROBERTSON, from Lochinver, started at the pottery last year. He mixes clay and packs the biscuit kilns.

SUSIE MACRAE has been with the company since 1990. She works part-time on the extruding and finishing.

DAWN HEALEY joined Highland Stoneware this year and is working in the extruding team and is training in other areas.

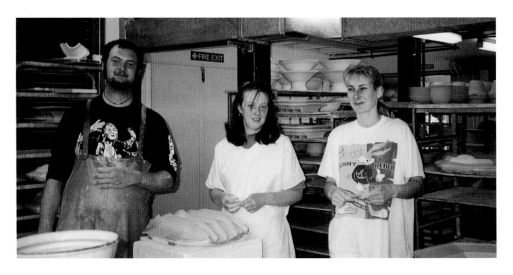

MAP

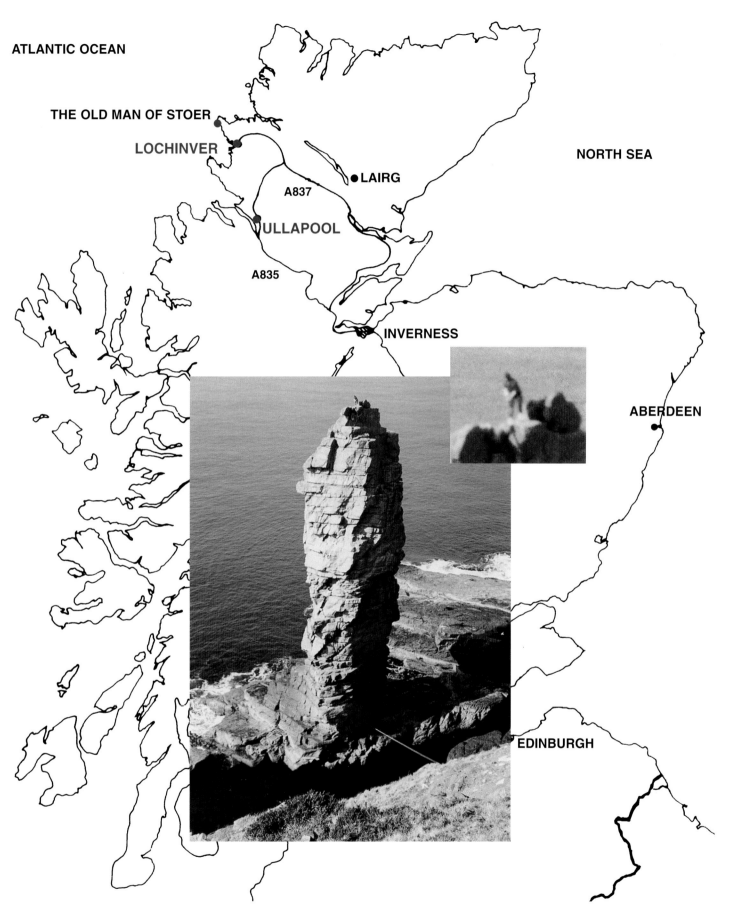

ATLANTIC OCEAN

THE OLD MAN OF STOER

LOCHINVER

NORTH SEA

A837

LAIRG

ULLAPOOL

A835

INVERNESS

ABERDEEN

EDINBURGH

Intrepid Highland Stoneware decorator, Pippa Peacock, on the summit of the Old Man
of Stoer with her climbing companion, Richard Baines.

MARKS

The stoneware marks are rubber-stamped with ink pads. The dates indicate the period of use although irregularities may occur. Stamps are made in three sizes. An annual stamped date code was introduced in April 1998 – **Q**– until April 1999 **R** – from April 1999.

1   1975 – current, now used only on smaller pieces

2   As number 1 but with the name of a tableware pattern c1978-1985

3   designed by Grahame Clarke c1978 – c1982

4   1986 – 1994

5   1994 – March 1998

6   Current mark as number 5 but with impressed thrower's mark, painter's monogram and date code **R** for 1999

7   Mark found on vases and mugs made for Highland Stoneware's 25th anniversary in 1999

DECORATORS AND THROWERS MARKS

Decorators' monograms have been painted on the base of giftware and tableware since 1998; and throwers' marks impressed on vases since 1998.

The dates listed indicate the year that the decorator or thrower joined the company.

Decorator	Year		Decorator	Year	
Audrey Paton	1991		Pippa Peacock	1993	
David Grant	1974		Rae Phipps	1975	
Paul Phipps	1975		Ruth Goldie	1988	
Dawn Chapman	1998		Steve Patterson	1997	
Dorell Pirie	1987		Tracey Montgomery	1992	
Fiona Mackay	1996		John Wood and thrower	1989-1998	
Heather Wallace	1997		Linda MacLeod	1976	
Lesley Thorpe	1989		Susan Brown	1999	

THROWERS

Thrower	Year
Fergus Stewart	1997
Paul Gow	1998
Steven Patterson	1997